THE GOSPEL IN REVELATION

Also by Graeme Goldsworthy

GOSPEL AND KINGDOM:
A Christian Interpretation of the Old Testament

THE GOSPEL IN REVELATION

Gospel and Apocalypse

GRAEME GOLDSWORTHY M.A., Th.D.

Centre for
Faith and Spirituality
Loughborough University

The Paternoster Press

First published 1984 by
The Paternoster Press, Paternoster House,
3 Mount Radford Crescent, Exeter, Devon
and
Lancer Books, P.O. Box 115,
Flemington Markets, New South Wales, NSW 2129

SOUTH AFRICA:
Oxford University Press, P.O. Box 1141, Cape Town

Passages from The Holy Bible, New International Version
Copyright © 1978 by New York International Bible Society.
First published in Great Britain 1978, used by permission of the
New York International Bible Society.

British Library Cataloguing in Publication Data

Goldsworthy, Graeme
The Gospel in Revelation
1. Bible. N.T. Revelation—Commentaries
I. Title
228'.06   BS2825.3

ISBN 0-85364-381-4

Australian ISBN 0-85892-250-9

Set in 11pt English Times by Busby Typesetting & Design, Exeter
and printed by A. Wheaton & Co. Ltd., Exeter, for
the publishers.

DEDICATED
TO ALL WHO SUFFER PERSECUTION
FOR THE SAKE OF CHRIST,
AND ESPECIALLY TO THE CHRISTIANS
IN SOVIET-OCCUPIED ESTONIA.

*Ja nemad on tema
võitnud Talle vere tõttu
ja oma tunnistuse sõna tõttu ...*

Ilmutuse 12:11
(Revelation 12:11)

Contents

Preface

This book is not a commentary and it is not intended to compete with the already large amount of commentary on the text of the Book of Revelation that is readily available. It is largely the outcome of my own attempts to expound the essential, contemporary message of Revelation in three separate Bible Study groups and in a series of public lectures at a Bible College. These expositions took place within a period of some nine or ten years and each lasted about three or four months. Within that period I was prompted from time to time to reflect on the broad plan and purpose of Revelation in relation to the overall pattern of biblical revelation. Exposition in informal groups permitted much useful dialogue with other Christians about how Revelation spoke to our real life situations. Perhaps it was also inevitable that my own keen interest in the Christian significance of the Old Testament should lead me to that book which not only contains more Old Testament quotations than any other book of the New Testament, but which also preserves the Old Testament literary idioms and thought patterns in a way unparalleled in the New Testament. I am grateful to those colleagues and friends who read the manuscript at various stages, and who made helpful suggestions and encouraged me. I am especially indebted to Mrs. Ellenor Neave for typing the manuscript.

GRAEME GOLDSWORTHY,
St. Stephen's Anglican Church,
Coorparoo, Brisbane.

Introduction: Principles of Interpretation

The Key to Understanding Revelation

The Book of Revelation seems to occupy one of two positions in most people's affections. Either it is almost totally neglected or it is elevated to a prominence shared by no other biblical book. As to the former position, the reasons are not hard to imagine. Apart from the letters to the seven churches in Chapters 2 and 3, the book is almost entirely given over to exotic and florid literary forms. The weird visions coupled with the constant use of Old Testament images and ideas, put the book in the "too hard" category for many ordinary readers. Few Christians today are used to reflecting on their existence and its meaning in terms of seven-headed beasts and apocalyptic horsemen. Since the idioms of Revelation are so strange to us we tend rather to concentrate on those parts of the New Testament which come to us in the straight-forward forms of letters and narratives.

Neglect of Revelation is also, paradoxically, related to the fact that there are those who seem to give it undue prominence. When the modern prophets and futuristic gurus have finished their extraordinary explanation of every visionary detail, and have mapped out the most complex chain of events due to start just about any time now, the ordinary reader is frightened almost out of his wits. His fright is not so much caused by the awful events that are imminent, but by the measure of expertise required to interpret the intricacies of this unusual and unfamiliar book. Better leave it to the specialists! And, of course, it works the other way too. By vacating the interpretative arena pastors, teachers, and their flocks leave a vacuum which looks very inviting to someone who desires the prophet's mantle. To be an expert on "things to come" is a sure way to fame (and sometimes fortune).

Certain habits of Bible reading are also risky in this matter. The commendable habit of daily reading of the Bible can easily become hardened into a set of rules on how we deal with the text. The practice of meditation on short passages is often productive but always open to danger. Short passages, by definition, are usually isolated passages cut loose from their wider context. This can cause misunderstanding as to the meaning of the passage even when it appears clear and beneficial as it stands. It can also cause perplexity. How does one meditate on the description of an apocalyptic monster? What encouraging thought for the day does the destruction of one third of the world's rivers provide? What is the message from the Lord to me in the catalogue of precious stones adorning the foundations of the heavenly city? Better leave well alone! Let the specialists deal with Revelation while we meditate on the clearer passages of the New Testament.

I once sat, very patiently I thought, while a caller to my home explained at very great length how all the events of contemporary world history gave out the unmistakable signal that the second coming of Christ was very near. The exposition was ingenious, and gave the message of Revelation a note of urgency. But there was a problem in it for me which I still cannot avoid. The urgency belonged wholly to *now*, to the last part of the twentieth century. Why, then, was John so urgent some nineteen hundred years before this? What was the *contemporary* meaning of that revelation which made the author of the book a concerned messenger of God writing to a small and persecuted minority of Christians in a hostile pagan world? If he wrote out of the agony of his own exile on Patmos, addressing specific churches in Asia Minor by name, what relevance to them was to be found in far-off events belonging, according to our modern prophets, to the nuclear-technological age?

Of course the New Testament has much to say about certain events of the future. The return of Christ, the resurrection of the dead, and the consummation of the kingdom of God are all future events. Furthermore, few commentators would dispute that the Book of Revelation speaks of these events. Insofar as John refers to these events and makes them relevant to his own day, he points to the fact that it is not *when* these will happen, but rather *what* it is that happens, which constitutes the urgency. These events, many of them future, were not given contemporary significance by John and other biblical authors by dating them in their lifetime, or in that of their readers. The New Testament writers probably had varying ideas about when the appearance of Christ in majesty would occur. But they all agreed on one thing, and that was that the first advent of Christ had brought all time and history into crisis. We can see this in the way they regard all time which follows the life, death and resurrection of Jesus as *end time*. About this I shall have more to say later on. Suffice it to say that, according to the New Testament, the gospel event of Jesus Christ throws all succeeding history into a new light. Whether men acknowledge it or not, the coming of Christ to live, die, and rise again, is the goal of all history. God not only created all things through Christ and for Christ (Colossians 1:16), but it was his eternal plan to bring all things to their fullness in Christ (Ephesians 1:9f) and that in the fullness of time (Galatians 4:4).

Principles of Interpretation

In talking about principles of interpretation, I do not want to give the impression that there is some *secret* key which unlocks all. There is a key, but it is not a secret. Nor do I want to suggest that it is a wholly technical matter which removes interpretation from the grasp of the simple minded and the theologically untrained. All disciplines and specialization of interest have some technical terms. A housewife tells me that she is a simple person and not up to any theological technicalities, and then turns without a thought to operate the latest in sewing machine gadgetry, or to interpret without a mistake a knitting pattern which makes Egyptian hieroglyphics pale into insignificance. A man tells me he is uneducated and not able to understand anything beyond the "simple gospel", and then proceeds to tune a car engine with the aid of some very sophisticated electronics. More often than not, it is unfamiliarity which daunts us rather than inherent difficulty. If we are motivated, most of us can and do come to grips with technical terms and abstract ideas.

There are two main principles of interpretation which come from the nature of the Bible itself. These have to do with the literary characteristics of the text and with the theological structures of the whole Bible.

1. Literary idiom[1]

The subject matter will frequently dictate the kind of literary expressions that are used in recording it. However, there is also a range of options open to any writer as to how he treats his material. An account of some significant historical event is probably best dealt with in straight historical narrative. But it is also possible to record it in the form of an epic poem or even to clothe it in symbolical language. Each idiom may convey the truth, but it will do so with distinctive shades of meaning and emphases. It is the task of the writer to strive to communicate what he sees as the truth of the matter in the idiom he believes to be best suited for his purpose. The reader's task is to penetrate to the writer's meaning. Straightforward prose description usually presents least problems because it most closely approximates to the general idiom of the day-to-day speech which we all use. In this twentieth century, poetry is usually a medium in which only a few feel at home. If a preacher were to deliver his sermon in poetic form he might well be dismissed as obscure. But the prophets of Israel, it would appear, regularly did just that, for most of their recorded sermons are in poetry. One can only presume that the average Israelite was much more accustomed to dealing with poetry as a medium of communication than we are.

1. *Idiom* means use of language in a way distinct to a particular person or group. It can also mean, as it does here, one of a number of acceptable ways in which words are used to convey the one idea.

Thus, when we are reading the Bible, or any other ancient literature, we are likely to find that there is a considerable gap between our modern literary methods and those of the ancient author. We cannot ignore this gap and pretend it isn't there. On the other hand let us not be discouraged. Much of this is a matter of being sensitive to the range of options open to any author. Sometimes we may need to dig a little into the background of some particular literary idiom in order to discover how it was used and with what intent. The Book of Revelation contains a number of different literary forms each with its own characteristics and functions. The most obvious are these:—

      a.   Letters
      b.   Prophetic oracles
      c.   Hymns of Praise
      d.   Apocalyptic Visions[2]

The principle of interpretation which emerges from this is that we must allow the author to use the literary conventions that exist for him in his time and culture, and to use them in the way that will suit his purpose. Most of the time the distinctive biblical idioms are so familiar to us that we accommodate ourselves to them without giving the matter a second thought. Often the idioms will be familiar to us in their biblical setting, as part of biblical literature, but unfamiliar to us in their original cultural setting. For example, most Christians will not find any difficulty with Jesus' words, "I am the good shepherd" or "I am the door of the sheep" (John 10). We have heard them often and we appear to comprehend them. But one day we hear an exposition of John 10 in which the cultural and historical background of ancient near eastern methods of keeping sheep are described. Suddenly the details of the passage take on a depth of meaning which we had never realized was there.

2. Most readers will be familiar with Revelation and the visions which are there in abundance. If, however, you are not sure what is meant by the term "apocalyptic vision", I suggest you read a couple now, eg. Daniel 7 and Revelation 13.

The doctrine of the inspiration of the Bible is extremely important but we must not misunderstand it. When John wrote under the inspiration of the Holy Spirit he was still John. He continued to think and to express himself in the thought forms and language patterns that were characteristically his. Inspiration did not suspend the human personality but worked through it. Thus when John chose, under the Spirit's inspiration, to write using the common literary forms of his day, he wrote according to the rules and conventions of a first century Jew. Our task in interpretation is to learn to recognize the different ways in which a first century Jew would write and how the different kinds of written expression function. The fact that the Jews developed a popular style of religious writing using a fairly standard kind of reported vision does not detract from John's visions, nor does it call into question the truth of his claims to have had such visions.

One further thing needs to be said here. Some forms of literary expressions are less familiar to us than others. The twentieth century mind can cope more easily with letters and straight narrative than with apocalyptic visions. There has been a lot of attention paid to this apocalyptic material in recent times by biblical scholars.[3] But, it is still very mystifying to the ordinary person. Added to this is the fact that apocalyptic visions, while often employing symbolic features which are frequently used and easily recognizable to the person familiar with them, nevertheless may contain symbolisms which are either deliberately ambiguous or else obscured by our distance from them. When we encounter such difficulties in the biblical material, particularly when some background information still fails to yield a clear meaning, there is a simple principle that applies. We must allow the clearer texts to take precedence over the more obscure. In practical terms, we cannot allow a point of

3. Commentaries on Revelation by H.B. Swete and R.H. Charles were published early this century. These could be regarded as monumental works in the English language. In more recent times a number of books have appeared on the subject of apocalyptic literature in general e.g. D.H. Russell, *Apocalyptic: Ancient and Modern* (Philadelphia: Fortress Press, 1978); Leon Morris, *Apocalyptic* (London: IVF, 1972).

doctrine to be established on an apocalyptic vision against clear statements to the contrary in the epistolary material of the New Testament (i.e. the Letters).

2. The centrality of the gospel

Our second principle of interpretation is often the most neglected, and yet it is absolutely basic to proper understanding. Simply stated this principle is that the gospel of Jesus Christ is the key to the interpretation of the whole Bible.[4] That is, Jesus Christ in his person and work, gives the meaning to the whole Bible. The New Testament states this principle in a number of different ways and, of course, applies it constantly. For example, when Paul says that the gospel is the power of God for salvation to everyone who believes (Romans 1:16), he means the whole of salvation, not just our introduction to it through initial conversion. Salvation, for Paul, is the salvation of the whole person, and it is the fullness of salvation. Part of our being saved by the gospel is the saving of our minds, our understanding. "Be transformed by the renewing of your minds" (Romans 12:2). How does the gospel "save" our minds? First, it does so by putting us on the same side as God so that we want to think his thoughts after him. We want to know his will and understand his Word. Secondly, the actual content of the gospel event shows to us the goal of all God's revealed purposes. So the Bible presents a unity of God's action for our salvation, first in the shadows of the Old Testament history and prophetic word, and then as the solid reality in Jesus Christ. One of the main aims of this book is to examine how the gospel interprets the Book of Revelation.

As we apply this principle to the Book of Revelation it will be not only because the gospel is evident within that Book. It is vital with Revelation, as with all the books of the Bible, that we do not treat it in isolation. The visions of Revelation must be read in the light of the unified message of the Bible which reaches its goal in Jesus Christ. There is one particular

4. This matter has been dealt with in some detail in my book *Gospel and Kingdom* (Exeter: The Paternoster Press, 1981; Minneapolis: Winston Press, 1982).

line of interpretation which does not follow this principle. It sees Revelation as answering to many of the prophecies of the Old Testament, but in such a way that neither these prophecies, nor Revelation are integral to the gospel. The gospel is not totally dissociated from these parts of the Bible, but it is nevertheless regarded as an intrusion into the process of the fulfilment of the prophecies in such a way as to suspend the process. Only after the gospel has run its appointed course in the world will the process of prophetic fulfilment be resumed. Such a view seems to ignore the New Testament's own testimony that the gospel is not a digression from prophetic fulfilment but rather the very essence of it.

What about the Millennium?

From the outset I wish to state my belief that the millennium is not the central theme of Revelation. The explicit references to Christ's reign of a thousand years are confined to one passage in the whole of the Bible: Revelation 20:1-10. Unfortunately, the specific interpretation of this passage has often been made the test of orthodoxy. I have tried to handle the subject in a way which neither gives it unwarranted prominence nor dismisses it as unworthy of serious consideration.[5] I see the millennium as only one of many pieces of imagery which contribute to the overall pattern of John's revelation. My aim has been to deal with it in a manner consistent with the interpretative principles which I have just outlined.

Perhaps one significant aspect of the ongoing debate about the millennium is that it serves to highlight different approaches to interpretation. Thus, the subject can be a fruitful area for the study of hermeneutical or interpretative method. What we should not wish to see, in my opinion, is this brilliant portrayal of the end of the conflict between Christ and Satan being made a perpetual battle ground and the cause of conflict between Christians.

5. There is plenty of literature on the subject for those who wish to pursue it, e.g.: L. Boettner, *The Millennium* (Philadelphia: The Presbyterian and Reformed Publishing Company, 1964); R. Clouse, *The Meaning of the Millennium* (Downers Grove: Inter Varsity Press, 1977; W.J. Grier, *The Momentous Event* (London: Banner of Truth, 1970).

The uninitiated may be rather irritated by distinctions between the premillennial, postmillennial and amillennial positions.[6] If so, they will probably identify with a jocular comment of a friend of mine who claims to be a panmillennialist because he is sure "it is all going to pan out in the end!" However, it is important to realise that most commentaries on Revelation come down on one or other position in the millennial debate simply because a particular view seems to the author to be in accord with his overall interpretation of the book. For example, one of the best introductory commentaries, in my view, is *I saw Heaven Opened* by Michael Wilcock.[7] There is no doubt as to Wilcock's amillennial position, but his work should not be judged purely on that basis. The reader will no doubt easily discern my general position on the millennium, but I hope that these few comments will encourage perseverance in those whose views differ from mine on this point, and in those who have little interest in the narrower confines of the debate. It is my hope that *The Gospel in Revelation* will lay the foundations for a more detailed study with the aid of a good commentary.

6. Premillennialism anticipates Christ's return before a literal thousand year reign on earth. Postmillennialism interprets the millennium as symbolic of a period in which the world becomes largely christianized, after which Christ returns. Amillennialism is similar to postmillennialism in that Christ returns after the millennium. The millennium is symbolic of this whole present age in which the gospel is preached. Unlike postmillennialism, amillennialism does not look for a golden age of gospel ascendancy as a prerequisite of the return of Christ. Unlike premillennialism, it does not look for a literal reign of Christ on earth for a period of one thousand years. (Figure 1 on p.20 illustrates these three views).

7. London: Inter Varsity Press, 1975, an amillennial treatment. The reader will also find the following useful: Leon Morris, *Revelation*, Tyndale New Testament Commentaries (London: Tyndale Press, 1969).

Fig. 1 THREE VIEWS ABOUT THE MILLENNIUM

Premillennialism

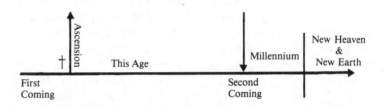

Postmillennialism

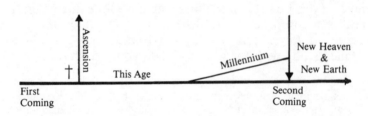

Amillennialism

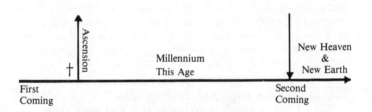

1

'I saw a Lamb standing as though it had been slain'

The Gospel as the Key to Revelation

Then I saw in the right hand of him who sat on the throne a scroll with writing on both sides and sealed with seven seals. And I saw a mighty angel proclaiming in a loud voice, "Who is worthy to break the seals and open the scroll?" But no-one in heaven or on earth or under the earth could open the scroll or even look inside it. I wept and wept because no-one was found who was worthy to open the scroll or look inside. Then one of the elders said to me, "Do not weep! See, the Lion of the tribe of Judah, the Root of David, has triumphed. He is able to open the scroll and its seven seals."

Then I saw a Lamb, looking as if it had been slain, standing in the centre of the throne encircled by the four living creatures and the elders.

And they sang a new song:

"You are worthy to take the scroll and to open the seals, because you were slain, and with your blood you purchased men for God from every tribe and language and people and nation" (Revelation 5:1-6,9).

The Lamb and the Lion

Apocalyptic was a form of religious writing that became very popular amongst the Jews from about the second century B.C. One of its characteristics was that the visionary related how he received a revelation from God (Apocalypse comes from the Greek word for revelation), and was then told to write it in a scroll and seal it until the time for revealing should come. The publication of the scroll would mean that the time had come and the secrets were out! John recalls this characteristic in Revelation 5. The scroll contains the message of God, the truth about his kingdom. But who is able to reveal it? John weeps because none is found who is worthy to reveal the truth about God and his kingdom and, so it seems, it must remain sealed in the scroll. But then he is given good news. There is one who has triumphed and is therefore able to open the scroll. He is the Lion of the tribe of Judah, the Messiah from the royal line of David. In that brief description John captures the sense of fierce majesty and irresistible strength. Here is repesented the warrior-king fresh from battle with the blood of the foe upon his sword. He is invincible and glorious in his conquests. He has filled with terror all who would resist him, and has put them to flight. Because of this power and might which has brought him triumph, the Lion is able to open to all men the mysteries of the kingdom of God.

But when John turns to see the Lion he sees no such figure of glory and majestic power. Rather he sees a Lamb standing "as though it had been slain". Even that verbal conundrum, so typical of apocalyptic, only heightens the effect which is to shatter the visual image of the Lord of the beasts. A slain Lamb! That is the victory which overcomes and puts the truth of the kingdom of God within our reach. By a skilful use of apocalyptic images, John illuminates the central paradox of the gospel. The victory of God was the humiliation and death of his Son. The Lion assumes the meekness of the Lamb and dies in order to overcome. Now the scroll can be opened and the voice is heard in praise:

"You are worthy to take the scroll and to open the seals,
because you were slain ..."

Through his suffering and death the Lamb is the revealer
of God. Appropriately the book is entitled "The Revelation
of Jesus Christ". Here we see that the key to the truth, all the
truth, about the kingdom of God is Jesus Christ in his life,
death and resurrection. John has woven this fact into the
apocalyptic idiom by depicting the slain Lamb as the one who
alone is worthy to unlock the truth. In this way John reminds
us of the centrality of the gospel in his book. If we would
unlock the meaning of Revelation it must be by means of the
fact that Jesus Christ in his earthly ministry of redemption is
the true and revealing Word of God. Revelation, like every
other book in the New Testament is an exposition of the
gospel. It may emphasize certain implications of the gospel,
but it is about the gospel just the same. As Michael Wilcock
says of the author:

> And now he was again to receive the Word and the
> Witness, a genuine message from God, which in due
> course was to be read aloud in Church meetings like
> other inspired scripture. It would in a sense be nothing
> new; simply a recapitulation of the Christian faith he
> possessed already. But it was to be the last time that
> God would repeat the patterns of truth, and he was to
> do so with devastating power and in unforgettable
> splendour.[1]

What is the Gospel?

Let us be clear what we mean by the centrality of the
gospel. First, what is the gospel? The gospel is the message
about Jesus Christ; about his life, death and resurrection for
us and our salvation. It is an historic thing in that Christ
redeemed us by what he was and did nearly two thousand
years ago in Palestine. While the effects of the gospel events
stretch both backwards and forward in time, those effects are

---

1. *I Saw Heaven Opened* (London: Inter-Varsity Press, 1975) p.31.

not themselves the gospel which we believe for our salvation.
It is important that we distinguish the effects or fruits of the
gospel from the gospel itself. Regeneration, faith and sanctification in the Christian are fruits of the gospel. But we do
not lay hold of our salvation by faith in faith, or in regeneration, or in the giving of the Holy Spirit. Only by faith in
Christ, in his living and dying as my substitute Man, do I
receive the gift of salvation. Even the second coming of
Christ is not the gospel, but a fruit of the gospel. We are not
saved by believing that he *will* come, but by believing that he
has come in the flesh for us.

So, the gospel is distinctly the work of Jesus Christ in a way
that it is not distinctly the work of God the Father or the Holy
Spirit. It is a perfect and a complete work which took place in
the very person of Jesus of Nazareth, and therefore not in us.
It, and it alone, is the basis of our acceptance with God. In
the writings of Paul, this latter fact is often spoken of as justification. To justify is to declare someone to be just or righteous. Because of the merits of Christ our substitute, God is
able to credit the believing sinner with those same merits. He
justifies the sinner purely on the basis of the fact that there is
one who stands as righteous in the sinner's place. The sinner
who believes is the sinner who trusts in the historic Christ as
his or her substitute before God. This historic Christ is alive
now at the right-hand of God. But he is there now as our substitute only because he was that historic substitute for us in
his life and death.

When we speak of the centrality of the gospel we refer to
the fact that every aspect of our salvation stems from the
gospel. We mean that the gospel is truly the power of God for
salvation in that it is through the gospel we are called, regenerated, converted, sanctified and finally glorified. We mean
that Jesus Christ, God come in the flesh, as he lived, died and
rose again, gave meaning to all history and human existence.
We mean that the gospel is the only means we have of
beginning, continuing and persevering in the Christian life.

The error that we must emphatically repudiate is the often
held notion that the gospel is the power of God only to get us
converted. I once heard a missionary speaker report how a
pastor in the mission field wrote to headquarters concerning

his flock: "We all know the gospel here, and now we must go on to something more solid." The idea is that the gospel is the gateway to Christian experience, and thus to eternal life, but once we enter that gateway we move on to another more solid reality by which we progress. Sanctification, or becoming holy, or growing in the Christian faith, is frequently depicted as a new stage after conversion. The means to it is variously presented. For some it is by an act of "total commitment", or of "self emptying" or of "putting to death the old nature". For others it is a distinct crisis experience of the Holy Spirit. Christian literature and preaching is full of "steps to the deeper life" or "keys to the abundant and victorious life". This is not to quibble over pious jargon and terminology. The point at issue is simply this. When we approach sanctification as attainable by any means other than the gospel of Christ—the same gospel by which we are converted—we have departed from the teaching of the New Testament.

The Centrality of the Gospel

The centrality of the gospel can be expressed with regard to any aspect of the biblical teaching of salvation. It means that what God achieved in Christ is the goal of all God's purposes as they are expressed in both Old and New Testaments. In this lies the meaning of Christ as Alpha and Omega.

1. Christ is the meaning of creation

We do not fully grasp the biblical teaching on creation until we have dealt with those passages that speak of Christ in creation. John 1:1-2 reminds us that the Word that became flesh as Jesus of Nazareth was the agent of creation. Paul takes this a step further in Colossians 1:15-20. Here Christ is spoken of as the one *in* whom, *through* whom and *for* whom all things were created. Let us be content at this stage to note that Paul is saying that the Christ who made peace by the blood of his cross (Colossians 1:20) is the agent, purpose and goal of creation. Some may think of the gospel as a kind of afterthought of God's which he devised when sin ruined the creation. But here we see that the gospel was God's fore-thought to creation. God created the heavens and the earth with the express plan and purpose of bringing all things to their ultimate goal through the suffering and death of Christ.

2. *Christ is the meaning of the Old Testament covenants and law*

The Old Testament sets out in great detail the fact that it was God's will to relate to his people in a specific way. In the redemptive process God relates to man in covenant. The covenant is a constitution which sets out the nature of the relationship between God and Israel, his chosen people. The law of Moses is the most comprehensive expression of this covenant relationship which is established through the gracious redemptive work of God. The New Testament picks up the covenant theme and speaks of Jesus Christ as the one who fulfils it. His birth brings to fruition all the covenant promises of the Old Testament (see Luke 1:46-55, 68-79, 2:29-32). That Jesus fulfilled the law (Matthew 5:17) means that he lived as the perfect covenant partner with God. In other words, he was without sin. His baptism at the hands of John the Baptist was the perfect expression of the human choice to live for God and not against him. And it was at his baptism that Jesus was declared to be God's true and beloved Son. Luke's use of the genealogy at this point (Luke 3:22-38) shows that the statement, "You are my Son", denotes Jesus' acceptance before God as the true Israelite, the true man (Adam is the son of God, v. 38).

3. *Christ is the meaning of prophecy*

Speaking of the law and the prophets Jesus said, "I have not come to abolish them but to fulfil them" (Matthew 5:17). It is a mistake to see this reference to the prophets as meaning that Jesus fulfilled certain messianic predictions which are scattered throughout the prophetic writings. The statement is all inclusive and means that all that the prophets spoke is fulfilled in Christ. The prophetic word of judgment against sin is fulfilled in the death of Christ on the Cross. The promises of a new convenant, a new restored people of God, a new dwelling place of God amongst men, are all fulfilled in Christ. Furthermore they are fulfilled in the gospel event. About this I will have more to say in later chapters, for this is a contentious point and I want to state clearly what I mean by it. Let us, for the moment, observe Paul's conviction that the prophetic promises find their "Yes" in Christ (2 Corinthians 1:20). Paul expressed this in his sermon at Antioch when he said, "We tell you the good news: What God promised to our fathers he has fulfilled for us, their children, by raising up Jesus" (Acts 13: 32-33).

4. Christ is the meaning of Christian existence

"For to me, to live is Christ", said Paul (Philippians 1:21). The Christ that he refers to is the Christ described in Philippians 2, that is, the Christ that suffered in the flesh, and was exalted to the place of honour with God (Philippians 2:6-11). It is the Christ of the gospel who is Lord. For Paul, it is this Christ who gives life its only possible meaning. Christ does this by both revealing and by re-establishing, through his redemptive act, the true relationship between God and man, man and man, man and the creation. He does this in his own being, and in such a way that the sinner who believes God's word that this redemptive act is for him is given, as a free gift, the same status that Christ possesses by virtue of his sin-free obedience. We cannot say it better than to use Paul's words: "Christ, who is our life" (Colossians 3:4). By this Paul means that, as a consequence of his perfect life and death, everything that Christ is before God, he is FOR US. He is the sinless Son FOR US. He is the true covenant partner FOR US. He is the beloved FOR US. He is the righteous and holy one, the judged sinner, the new life, the Spirit-filled man, the perfect worshipper of God—all FOR US.

From this fact of the gospel existence of Christ FOR US, and from this fact alone, comes the motive and the power for our Christian existence. All the fruits of the gospel are just that: fruits *of the gospel*. Regeneration, faith, sanctification and final perseverance are all fruits of the gospel. They can grow on no other tree. Legalistic demands, cajolery, and brow-beatings for "deeper-commitment" and "total surrender", when cut loose from the grace of the gospel are but wretched weeds which can produce only despondency, disillusionment and rebelliousness.

5. Christ is the meaning of the second coming

The first coming of Christ, the gospel-event, establishes the significance of the second coming of Christ. Perhaps one of the greatest reasons for misunderstanding of the Book of Revelation is the failure to grasp the relationship of the first and second comings of Christ. Let us be very clear about this point. Christ does not return to do some new or different work. His return in glory will be to consummate the finished work of his life, death and resurrection. At his coming he will be revealed in all his glory to all principalities and powers. That which the believer now grasps by faith will be open to every eye. That which the believer now owns by faith and which is in Christ, his substitute, will be perfected as the reality in himself. The *status* that we now have in Christ will become the *state* we have in ourselves.

It is this relationship of the first and second comings which provides the structure of John's thought in the Book of Revelation. It is the relationship of the suffering Christ to the Christ who is manifested in glory. It is the relationship of the Lamb to the Lion. The Lion is the symbol of the majesty of the glorious messiah-king of Israel who is revealed in the glory of the kingdom of God. The Lamb is the symbol of the suffering Jesus of Nazareth. John shows us that he who would see the Lion must find him first in the Lamb. The messianic kingdom of Israel has its reality only through the redemptive work of the Christ who died and rose again. Although the Lamb will ever be the Lamb, for the glorified Christ is exalted on account of his sufferings, nevertheless the majesty of the Lion will shine forth from the Lamb at his second coming.

Living by Faith means Living by the Gospel

For the present the Lion's glory is veiled. Only faith can perceive it through the gospel. The testimony of the New

Testament to Jesus as the reigning Christ is one that can only be believed or rejected, for there is no objective proof of it. We can try to evaluate the records of the four Gospels with regard to the historic events of Jesus' life, death and resurrection. But, in the end, we cannot perceive that our salvation lies in those events other than by believing that it is so because God assures us that it is so. In the Gospels we read how people responded to Jesus in different ways. Some rejected him as a false prophet. Others were enthusiastic for him only so long as they thought he would free them from the Romans or supply their material needs. A few were enabled to perceive in him the answer to the true spiritual hopes of Israel. Even his closest friends misunderstood some of what he was saying to them. In fact we see that it is only when the Holy Spirit is given at Pentecost that the followers of Jesus finally understand what it was all about.

Paul describes this present existence of the believer as that of a nomadic tent-dweller:

> While we are in this tent we groan and are burdened, because we do not wish to be unclothed but to be clothed with our heavenly dwelling, so that what is mortal may be swallowed up by life. Now it is God who has made us for this very purpose and has given us the Spirit as a deposit, guaranteeing what is to come. Therefore we are always confident and know that as long as we are at home in the body we are away from the Lord. We live by faith, not by sight (2 Corinthians 5:4-7).

There is a real sense of our incompleteness in being away from the Lord. So we live by faith, not by sight. Faith is never a vaguely defined thing for Paul. It is always defined by its object: Jesus Christ. Faith means implicit trust in the Christ of the gospel to save and sustain us. To live by faith means to live by the gospel. Paul is saying that the Holy Spirit is given to us to guarantee the final participation of the believer in the kingdom where he will no longer be away from the Lord. How does the Holy Spirit act as this guarantee? He does so by enabling us to live by faith. The Spirit establishes our faith and trust in the living and dying of Jesus for us. The Spirit's work is to energize our faith, not in faith itself, nor in the

Spirit himself, but in Christ alone. While we are absent from the Lord we must know him as the historic Jesus of Nazareth who wrought salvation for us. By faith we know that this Saviour is now the Lion who has conquered, the ruling Lord of all creation. But we can know him thus only because of his conquest as the suffering Lamb.

These truths of our salvation and its effect on our present Christian existence are the commonplace of the New Testament. John has taken them once more and reclothed them in forms and images which are the coinage of the Old Testament. By doing this he fulfils a purpose which we will see is of great value to us. It is, as Austin Farrer[2] has described it, though a rebirth of images, the old images of a passing culture and people, that John surprises us with a fresh glimpse of the grandeur of God's plan. He thus saves the ordinary struggling Christian from a trivial view of himself and of his meaning. He enables us to see that the tribulation of the Lamb dignifies the tribulations, small and great, of every believer with a significance that can never be swallowed up in the chaos of meaninglessness.

Summary

The Lion is the image of the glorified and reigning Christ. He alone can unlock the kingdom of God to us and make its reality known. But, like John, we can see the Lion only as he has come to us in the form of the slain Lamb. John points to the gospel-event; the living, dying and rising of Jesus Christ, as the key to the revelation of the kingdom. It is thus also the key to the Book of Revelation. By the use of this figure, he points to the meaning of all existence as that which is revealed in the gospel. For the Christian there is a tension between the coming of the kingdom through the gospel and the continuation of the present order. Living by faith means living by the gospel. What this means is the subject of John's book.

THESIS
The Lamb-Lion tension shows that the gospel is the only key to the understanding of the Book of Revelation.

2. Austin Farrer, *A Rebirth of Images* (London: A. & C. Black, 1949).

2

'The tribulation and the kingdom'

The Gospel and Our Present Sufferings

I, John, your brother and companion in the suffering and kingdom and patient endurance that are ours in Jesus, was on the island of Patmos because of the word of God and the testimony of Jesus. On the Lord's day I was in the Spirit, and I heard behind me a loud voice like a trumpet, which said: "Write on a scroll what you see and send it to the seven churches" (Revelation 1:9-11).

The Occasion of the Book

One of the neglected aspects of Revelation in many modern interpretations of it is the occasion of its writing. We should never lose sight of the historic circumstances out of which this extraordinary book arose. For our purposes it is not important to determine whether or not the author is the apostle John or some other. Nor does an exact dating really matter. John describes the background circumstances sufficiently to enable us to appreciate the purpose of the book. John is in exile on the little Aegean isle of Patmos because of his active

Christian witness. He writes a circular letter to a group of churches across on the mainland of Asia Minor (what is now the eastern part of Turkey). In it he expresses his solidarity with these Christians who are also undergoing hardship because of persecutions. He comforts, encourages, chides, and exhorts them in the gospel. He reminds them of the meaning of Christ's sufferings and of his glory, that they might stand firm in the knowledge that their own sufferings are utterly consistent with the reality of God's kingdom in this present age. At a time when many Christians were possibly quite literally running for their lives, he does not detain them with a closely argued theological treatise. Rather he draws from the familiar and fertile imagery of Jewish apocalyptic in order to paint vivid word-pictures of the reality of the kingdom of God. They are images that will stick in the mind and aid the recall of the basic truths of the gospel. They are images that use bold strokes and brilliant colours to represent the victory of the kingdom of God over the powers of darkness. In the extremity of suffering when the details of a Pauline exposition of justification by faith may be difficult to recall, the simple and unlettered Christian would more easily remember what had been read to him in the assembly about the slain Lamb glorious upon his throne.

As John wrote these words, he, along with so many of his fellow-Christians, was experiencing the hard reality of the words of Jesus to his disciples: "In the world you have tribulation" (John 16:33). This tribulation included martyrdom for many Christians in the first and second centuries. But even in times of relative calm, life for the believer was full of pressures, conflicts and bewildering circumstances. When the Church came under exceptional pressure from the pagan world, and met fierce opposition, many a believer paid for his faithfulness with his life. Then the Church cried out, as did the psalmist of old, "How long O Lord?" (Psalm 79:5, Revelation 6:10).

John does not urge his fellow-Christians to seek a means of escape from this tribulation, for he understood only too well that discipleship means suffering. Rather he urges them to persevere to the end and so to receive the blessings prepared for them. Patience, endurance, perseverance and overcoming are not impossible ideals which John uses in a vain and desperate bid to keep a persecuted minority from ultimate disillusionment. They are the realities of the kingdom of God as it breaks into our history and gathers its members towards the great consummation. They are born of the truth which is in Jesus himself: "In the world you have tribulation, but be of good cheer, I have overcome the world" (John 16:33 RSV).

Once we have looked at John's purpose in this way, we are in a position to express the abiding truth and application of the Book of Revelation to ourselves in the twentieth century. The paradox of the Lamb and the Lion is translated into Christian existence when John speaks of "the suffering and kingdom and patient endurance that are ours in Jesus" (Revelation 1:9). These are the two dimensions of our present struggle. Christian existence is lived out between the two realities of suffering and the kingdom. It reflects the suffering of the Lamb and anticipates the consummation of the kingdom through the conquest of the Lion.

The cause of all suffering

Suffering is the abiding experience of Christians. That may sound rather trite coming from the context of the affluence of western society and of the freedom of religious expression. In the non-communist world we are becoming more aware of the persecution of Christians in the Soviet Union and other Eastern bloc countries. We hear from time to time of the modern martyrs who really do come to the ultimate test of a faithful witness to Christ. Against these sufferings the hassles we face day by day fade almost to nothing. And yet people do suffer in the midst of political freedom and economic affluence. Suicides, divorce, mental illness, race riots and neglect of children are some of the more publicized problems of western society. Christians are immune from none of them.

Biblical reference to the suffering of Christians includes all of these and much more. Suffering is the direct result of the fall of man. Suffering comes from the dislocation of the true relationships for which God created us. The seeds of all

natural disasters such as earthquake, flood and famine, lie in
the fact that God cursed the earth on account of man:
"Cursed is the ground because of you; through painful toil
you will eat of it all the days of your life. It will produce
thorns and thistles for you, and you will eat the plants of the
field" (Genesis 3:17-18).

This connection between the fall of man and natural disasters may seem fanciful to some readers. It is established not
only on the basis of the scripture just quoted, but also on
Paul's assertion that "the creation was subjected to frus-
tration," and that "the creation itself will be liberated from
its bondage to decay and brought into the glorious freedom
of the children of God" (Romans 8:20,21).

Not only is man out of harmony with the creation, but also
with himself. Human relationships are ruined by sin in that
selfishness has replaced concern for others. While man
acknowledged his true creatureliness before God he could not
exalt himself above his brother. Now, other-centredness has
given way to self-centredness. The chief damage of sin is to
the relationship between God and man. Sin is our rejection of
God as Lord, and the desire to be lord of our own lives. All
other relationships depend on our relationship to God. When
the one is ruined all are ruined.

All the problems of contemporary society are but reflec-
tions of the basic dislocation of the relationship between man
and God. Because God has defined us at creation in relation
to himself, we are less than truly human when we are out of
that relation. Central to this relationship was man's "yes" to
his Creator. When Adam refused to affirm this relationship;
when he said "no" instead of "yes", God ceased to affirm
man and judged him.

Today this judgment is visible in the natural disasters, the
political upheavals, the personal tragedies, and the loneliness
of people in big cities. It is seen in greedy multi-national cor-
porations, dishonest business, power-hungry unionism, and
drunken driving. It is seen in cancer and birth defects, in the
neglect of minorities and the rejection of the aged. It is seen
in family conflict and social disturbance. It is seen in the
ravaging of earth's resources, in the pollution of air, water
and food. It is seen in decay and death. For all of this we and

the whole of mankind are collectively to blame, for all have sinned.

The suffering of the Christian

When a child of Adam is renewed through the gospel and made a member of the new humanity of which Christ is the head, a great deal changes. The believing sinner is the repentant sinner who seeks to forsake his former "no" to God. He believes the word of God about sin and the forgiveness which is through Christ. He hears the word of God which assures every believer of sonship freely given on the grounds of the perfect sonship of Jesus Christ. Consequently he wants to live as a son of God and begins the struggle against the world, the flesh and the devil. He longs for the return of Christ which will mean his own perfecting and entry into the final glory of the kingdom of God.

But while there are radical and immediate changes that take place for the sinner the moment he believes the gospel and trusts Christ for salvation, there are also many things that remain the same. The believer is not perfected in this life. He remains a sinner, though forgiven. He remains a sinner even though he seeks to eliminate sins. Conversion does not remove us from this world but rather puts us into conflict with it. Salvation is not instantaneous, and the reason is not hard to find. It has pleased God to bring in his kingdom through the gospel which must be preached throughout the world. We shall see later on that this is a perspective which is distinct to the New Testament and which modifies quite drastically the perspective of the Old Testament on the coming of the kingdom.

Thus the believer becomes a child of God, but remains a sinner. He becomes an inheritor of the new age, but remains a dweller in the old age. He receives eternal life but, unless Christ comes first, he will suffer sickness and death before he is resurrected to life. The Christian not only does not escape the woes of this sinful world, but he must also be content to lose favour with the world through non-conformity to its standards. Suffering then, is the norm of Christian experience. Far from removing suffering from us, becoming a

Christian compounds it. That is why we walk by faith and not by sight. That means that we live according to what we know by faith to be true—that we are the children of God and that our salvation is sure. It means that we do not live by what we experience. Reality cannot be gauged by what we feel or by the circumstances of our lives. What we now possess by faith is in Christ in heaven: "Your life is now hidden with Christ in God" (Colossians 3:3). That is why John says, "Now we are the children of God, and what we will be has not yet been made known. But we know that when he appears, we shall be like him, for we shall see him as he is" (1 John 3:2).

Paul's view of the matter is instructive. Suffering is a reality for there is a sense in which we share Christ's sufferings. Of course the church cannot suffer as Christ did in that he was the sinless one suffering for the sins of others. But the sufferings of Christ establish the nature of service or ministry in this world. While Christ's sufferings for us were unique, unrepeatable and infinite, yet there is a sense in which Christ must go on suffering in the world for the sake of the world. These sufferings he suffers in his body the church. Paul refers to his own sufferings thus: "I fill up in my flesh what is still lacking in regard to Christ's afflictions, for the sake of his body, which is the church" (Colossians 1:24). Again he said, "For just as the sufferings of Christ flow over into our lives, so also through Christ our comfort overflows" (2 Corinthians 1:5). Peter says: "Rejoice that you participate in the sufferings of Christ, so that you may be overjoyed when his glory is revealed... If you suffer as a Christian, do not be ashamed, but praise God that you bear that name" (1 Peter 4:13,16).

Paul has much to say about the matter in his letter to the Romans also: "We also rejoice in our sufferings, because we know that suffering produces perseverance; perseverance, character; and character, hope. And hope does not disappoint us, because God has poured out his love into our hearts by the Holy Spirit, whom he has given us" (Romans 5:3-5). Suffering is also the mark of true sonship: "... But you received the Spirit of sonship. And by him we cry, 'Abba, Father.' The Spirit himself testifies with our spirit that we are God's children. Now if we are children, then we are heirs—heirs of God and co-heirs with Christ, if indeed we share in his sufferings in order that we may also share in his glory. I consider that our present sufferings are not worth comparing with the glory that will be revealed in us" (Romans 8:15-18).

These scriptures are consistent in what they teach us. The church as the body of Christ, and therefore the individuals within it, suffers in the world. Suffering is not a sign that God has forsaken us but, on the contrary, it is one of the marks of true sonship. This suffering is the characteristic of our ministry which flows on from Christ's suffering ministry. But suffering is not without benefit and not without end. The end of Jesus' suffering, through his resurrection and glorification, points every Christian to his destiny of glorification. In the light of this destiny which Christ both secured for us and revealed to us in his earthly ministry, our present sufferings pale. It would be wrong to say that they pale into insignificance, for they are real and often very hard to bear. Furthermore, God in his goodness uses these very sufferings to shape our character and to fill us with hope for the true glory yet to be experienced. Even when our sufferings are culpable and self-inflicted through the hardness of our hearts, God graciously uses this for our ultimate good. Thus, "in all things God works for the good of those who love him, who have been called according to his purpose" (Romans 8:28).

We must reject any notion that becoming a Christian guarantees smooth sailing all the way through life. We do not minimize the resources of the Christian to cope with life. There is a very great difference between coping with life's hardships and "copping out" of them. With godly wisdom a Christian is able under "normal" circumstances to avoid those things which destroy the body, debase the mind, and seduce the soul. But being a Christian does not necessarily save him from shivering on a winter's night during a power blackout, or from the hazards of natural disasters and the drunken driver speeding through a red-light. Above all being a Christian means that we have taken sides in the final warfare between light and darkness. If God wills to bring in his kingdom through the preaching of the gospel, then all of us who own that gospel stand in the front line of battle. We must never underestimate the foe.

What John does for us in the Book of Revelation is to underscore not only the fact of suffering in the Christian life, but also the real source of it in the conflict between the kingdom of God and the kingdom of Satan.

Christ's Victory

The second dimension to Christian existence is established by the fact of Jesus Christ. Jesus said, "In the world you will have trouble. But take heart! I have overcome the world." The answer to tribulation was not to remove the believer from it, but assure him that the world has been overcome by Christ. To the sceptic who wants the acid-test of scientific proof, this seems a very pretentious statement. Look at the facts. The leader was popular for a while but was finally forsaken and done to death. His followers did indeed spread throughout the world, but at the times when they seemed most powerful they lacked most clearly the characteristics of love and servanthood that the leader spoke of. Today, the followers go on protesting that they believe in one holy universal church. In fact it is none of these things to the observer.

The error of the sceptic is not that he perceives the weakness and the sinfulness of the church, but that he tests the truth of the gospel by these marks. Those who are mesmerized by a temporary show of strength and grandeur in the church are likewise in danger of missing the truth. It was the error of some of Jesus' contemporaries that they misperceived the implications of the coming of the kingdom. The apparent contradiction between the prophetic predictions of a glorious Israel ruled by the Davidic prince before whom all nations bowed, and those of the suffering servant who was despised and rejected in order to bear the sins of many, was too much for them to accept. These Jews forgot the suffering servant and looked only for the conquering prince. The message of a crucified messiah thus became an obstacle, a stumbling block of offence. But this offensive figure is, says Paul, "the power of God, and the wisdom of God" (1 Corinthians 1:24).

The victory of Christ is the victory of his death and resurrection. In saying this, we do not separate these climactic events from the whole of Jesus' life. What is often called the active obedience of Christ, his perfect obedience to the law of God in his life, is integral with his passive obedience, his suffering and death. In his life Jesus displayed many signs of his victory as he exercised power over Satan's temptations, over demons, over natural forces, over material objects, over people's wills, over sickness and death. The miracles of Jesus were all signs of the arrival of the kingdom which had been heralded by the prophets of Israel.

The obedience of Christ culminated in his death on the cross. This, to the world's way of thinking, was the defeat of a pathetic dream. But God has declared this to be the decisive victory over Satan, sin and death. The hostility of sin was overcome and the rebellion of mankind overcome. "For God was pleased to have all his fullness dwell in him (Christ), and through him to reconcile to himself all things, whether things on earth or things in heaven, by making peace through his blood, shed on the cross" (Colossians 1:19-20). "And having disarmed the powers and authorities, he made a public spectacle of them, triumphing over them by the cross" (Colossians 2:15).

Summary

The two dimensions of the Christian life as John draws it, are the tribulation and the kingdom. In order to understand ourselves and the nature of Christian existence we need to understand these two dimensions and how they relate. Suffering is the common lot of humanity and not too hard to describe. Christians often need to learn, however, that their membership of the kingdom of God does not make them immune to sickness and suffering in this life. There is a tendency to make this error in some circles that stress the presence of miraculous phenomena, especially healings. The error is bred from a misperception of how the kingdom comes. In a real sense, this is the question to which Revelation addresses itself. The victory of Christ is real, for he has overcome the world. Until he comes, however, the Church must suffer in the world.

THESIS

The theme of the Lamb and the Lion points to the paradox of the normal suffering of Christians and the victory of Christ.

3

'They have washed their robes in the blood of the Lamb'

Justification by Faith in Revelation

> Then one of the elders asked me, "These in white robes—who are they, and where did they come from?" I answered, "Sir, you know." And he said, "These are they who have come out of the great tribulation; they have washed their robes and made them white in the blood of the Lamb" (Revelation 7:13-14).

The Christian's suffering is not forever. To think otherwise would make a mockery of the gospel and of the hope of glory. Tribulation belongs to this age in which there is a real sense of "not having". But, it is a transitory preparation for the time when the full glory is revealed. Because of our confidence in the reality of the perfect life beyond the resurrection, suffering is given a positive dimension. Paul tells us that, because of the gospel, suffering produces endurance, patience and hope (Romans 5:3-5).

The Christian view of this life and the life to come is defined by the person and work of Christ. Unfortunately, the on-going relevance of the gospel to our life-view is often forgotten by Christians. How many Christians can give a

41

credible statement on how we gain acceptance with God? Far too few. And even fewer seem to have any clear idea about how our acceptance with God relates to daily life and godly living. Furthermore, what has been described as "warm-bath" Christianity encourages the idea that the heart of the Christian message has to do with being able to live an unruffled existence. Such an approach leads in time to the obscuring of the real issue which the gospel forces upon us: "How can the sinner find acceptance with a righteous God?"

In order to answer this question biblically we must accept the Bible's answer. We must be prepared to come to terms with the kind of distinctions that the Bible makes in setting forth the work of God for our salvation. In Chapter 1 we saw that the gospel is the hub of all biblical teaching. It is the heart of the Christian message and permeates all Christian truth. It bears repeating that those who are impatient with the vital distinction between the gospel as the work of God FOR US in Jesus Christ, and the fruit of the gospel (sanctification) as the work of God IN US by his Spirit, will never grasp the meaning of the fact that the gospel is the central fact upon which all else hinges.

The Sovereignty of God in Salvation

Revelation 7 records the vision of John in which he sees the angelic agents of God's wrath. Another angel commands them to withhold the tribulation of judgment until the servants of God are marked with a protective seal. Then John says that he heard the numbers of those who were sealed: twelve thousand from each of the tribes of Israel. After this he sees another vision of an innumerable multitude from every nation, tribe and language, standing before the throne of the Lamb and praising him for their salvation. An elder standing by identifies the crowd as those who have washed their robes and made them white in the blood of the Lamb.

Let us not misunderstand John. He is not suggesting that the gospel delivers us immediately from tribulation. The time will come when we will be removed from all suffering forever. This view of final deliverance is intended to comfort us in our present sufferings by showing that no tribulation can over-whelm us and sweep us away from our place in the kingdom. Furthermore, the last great judgment of God on all sin and rebellion against his kingdom, will not touch those who are his. There is one tribulation that the believer will never experience, and that is the final visitation of God's wrath, and eternal death.

We notice also in this chapter of Revelation that John uses two distinct word pictures to express his meaning. In the first he portrays the sealing of a perfect number of the people of Israel. It is not his intention to refer to the literal nation of Israel. He has too frequently followed the other writers of the New Testament in applying the old Israelite terminology to the true people of God, the new Israel in Christ, to slip back into Jewish particularism. Nor is it John's intention to state that exactly 144,000, no more and no less, will inherit the kingdom. He is at home in the apocalyptic use of symbolic numbers and would not understand such crass literalism at all. No, John is saying that the gathering clouds of judgment will overtake the created order. The present suffering of the saints is not to be misunderstood as evidence that God can or will forget those that are his. The horrendous tribulation to come cannot threaten one single member of God's kingdom. All who are Abraham's children by faith in Jesus Christ (see Galatians 3:9) are secure from the wrath to come.

It is comforting to know that the number of God's elect is a perfect number. The kingdom of God will not lack one member that belongs to its perfection. Every place that Christ has gone to prepare (John 14:2-3) will be filled. God's pur-pose to establish his perfect kingdom cannot be thwarted by man or devil. God has established the number of the elect and their names have been written in the book of life from the foundation of the world (Ephesians 1:4, Revelation 13:8). This perfect number—the square of twelve by the cube of ten —speaks eloquently of the security of the believer. I hasten to add that the doctrine of the security of the believer or, as it is sometimes known, the perseverance of the saints, means the security of the *believer*. This is no "once saved, always saved" doctrine which allows one to ignore godliness and to sin freely on the basis of some alleged conversion experience.

Perseverance means perseverance in faith and well-doing. The Book of Revelation constantly urges perseverance as the continuing life of faith.

Some may object that to speak of election or predestination is to limit the kingdom of God to a few. Does it not make God a capricious tyrant? We must answer that such objections usually stem from a refusal to accept that we are faced here with a mystery that it is not given to us to solve. There is also a radical misunderstanding which maintains that God's sovereignty in election removes man's responsibility. Such is not true. How divine sovereignty and human responsibility work together we cannot know. The Bible makes it clear that they do.

Let us remember that Jesus discriminated and limited the numbers of the saved: "Small is the gate and narrow the road that leads to life, and only a few find it" (Matthew 7:13-14). This is in line with the Old Testament teaching that only a faithful remnant of Israel would be saved. The little remnant idea must be seen in its context of the history of Israel, for it does not mean that the kingdom will be very sparsely populated. Election must not be interpreted as the activity of a capricious God who wants to bar the masses from entry into heaven. In fact, it works the other way. Such is the nature of sinful man that without God's sovereign election heaven would be empty. It is the means by which God infallibly brings into the kingdom the perfect number out of the mass of humanity. Without it none would be saved.

John has a second picture which complements the first. This time it is not the perfect number of Israel that he sees, but the innumerable saints from every nation on earth. The church of God is truly catholic (universal), for while salvation came through one Man of one tribe of one nation, the kingdom will consist of people of every nation. This does not contradict Jesus' "few", nor the remnant idea of the Old Testament. Both concepts point to the exclusive office of Christ so that no-one comes to the Father except through him (John 14:6). For all that, the elect remnant of God will be a staggering multitude of people.

Now note the elder's description of these people that John sees. They have washed their robes in the blood of the Lamb.

The imagery is transparent. Cleansing from the pollution of sin is a well-worn biblical idea. The law of Moses contained many prescriptions for ritual and actual washing to symbolize a cleansing from sin.[1] Blood was used also in purification rites.[2] This shows the clear link between the sacrificial provisions of the law and the idea of cleansing from pollution. This was given constant expression in the Old Testament in the Prophets and the Psalms.[3] The imagery of cleansing also underwent some variation, for example, in the vision of Zechariah 3. Here the High Priest, representing Israel, stands clothed in filthy robes symbolizing Israel's pollution in the Babylonian exile. The High Priest is then clothed in pure garments as a sign of Israel's cleansing. Not unrelated is Jesus' parable of the wedding feast where one guest is found without a wedding garment (Matthew 22:1-14). Whatever the reason for this man's state of undress, he is judged unworthy and cast out. His own clothing is unfit for the feast. John himself has taken up this theme in Revelation 19, and we shall examine it in more detail later.

The common message in all these purification images is that the pollution of sin must be cleansed before one may enter God's holy kingdom. The New Testament applies the death of Christ to this need:

> The blood of Jesus, his Son, purifies us from every sin. (1 John 1:7)

> Since we have confidence to enter the Most Holy Place by the blood of Jesus ... let us draw near to God with a sincere heart in full assurance of faith, having our hearts sprinkled to cleanse us from a guilty conscience and having our bodies washed with pure water.
> (Hebrews 10:19,22)

---

1. Eg., Exodus 30:19; 40:31; Leviticus 8:6; 14:8; 15:5-10 and 19-27; 16:24; Numbers 19:19.
2. Eg., Leviticus 8:14-30; 14:6-8.
3. Eg., Psalms 26:6; 51:1-19; Isaiah 1:16-20; Jeremiah 2:22; 4:14; Haggai 2:10-19.

John shows us in his vision of the multitude of the saved that it is the blood of the atoning sacrifice of the Lamb that removes the pollution of sin (Revelation 7:14).

Pollution and guilt are closely related. The Bible does not depict the sinner as one who has accidentally picked up some filth through inadvertent contact with what is unclean. He is in fact utterly blameworthy for his defilement. He stands guilty and condemned. To be set right before God he must be purged of uncleanness and forgiven. Having said that, we must be careful to observe that the gospel way of forgiveness takes place on the basis of the perfect righteousness of Christ and his atoning death. In other words, for a sinner to be made righteous in himself, he must first of all be declared righteous by faith. The great transaction of justification on the grounds of Christ's merits is God's way of saving us. The justified sinner is the one whom God declares to be "not guilty". He does this on the basis of Christ's righteousness which he imputes, or credits, to the sinner who believes the gospel. The justified sinner is one who has received by faith the gift of the righteousness of Christ to clothe him before the searching eye of a holy God. He possesses by faith everything that belongs to Christ as God's true man. He is as acceptable to God as Jesus was when God called him "beloved Son" (Matthew 3:17).

This imputation to the sinner of a righteousness which is not his own, is not a legal fiction. It is a just transaction because the sinner's debt has been fully paid and God's justice is satisfied. It is also a loving transaction because the recipient never deserves such kindness. John is telling us in Revelation 7 that God's sealing of his saints and the washing of one's robe in the blood of the Lamb, amount to the same thing. The outcome is sure and so the believer is given a basis for full assurance of salvation.

Justification in Revelation

Justification is not an occasional theme in Revelation. It is in fact the very warp and woof of the book. The structure and message of Revelation is not based on a few spectacular events immediately preceding the second coming of Christ, but rather upon the historic facts of the gospel, the person and work of Jesus Christ. This is not so apparent at first sight because so much of the book describes various judgments which point toward the consummation of the kingdom. It would be foolish to deny that Revelation deals with eschatology[4], that is, with the things relating to the end. There is much eschatology in Revelation. It is however, important that we grasp the perspective of this eschatology, and its relationship to our present existence. Above all, we must recognize that eschatology is shaped and given its significance by the historic events of the gospel.

When we speak of justification we are using a formal or technical way of referring to the gospel and its meaning. Through the life and death of Jesus the believer is accounted by God as free from the guilt of sin, and is thus accepted by God as his child. It is this message that permeates all that John is saying to us in Revelation. We note that it was the preaching of this gospel which led to the occasion for the writing of Revelation. Thus from the beginning the historic events of the gospel stand at the centre of the message. This is the revelation of Jesus Christ made known to John who bore witness to the word of God and the testimony of Jesus (Revelation 1:1-2). In his initial greeting to the recipients of his message John identifies the source of all their salvation as Jesus Christ, who is the faithful witness, the firstborn from the dead, and the ruler of the kings of the earth. Here he refers to the life, death, resurrection and present Lordship of Christ.

John then goes on to speak of the effects of Christ's death using a familiar Old Testament idea:

> To him who loves us and has freed us from our sins by his blood, and has made us a kingdom and priests to serve his God and Father—to him be glory and power for ever and ever! Amen (Revelation 1:5b-6).

---

4. Greek: *eschatos*—last. Eschatology is the study of the last things.

This recalls the words of God to Moses on Mount Sinai as he spoke of the redemption of Israel from slavery in Egypt:

> You yourselves have seen what I did to Egypt, and how I carried you on eagles' wings and brought you to myself. Now if you will obey me fully and keep my covenant, then out of all nations you will be my treasured possession. Although the whole earth is mine, you will be for me a kingdom of priests and a holy nation (Exodus 19:4-6).

Israel was given this privileged position through the covenant by which the God of all the universe committed himself to one small and otherwise insignificant nation.

The use of the political model of a kingdom to describe Israel foreshadowed the time when the nation would be ruled by the royal dynasty of David. But this political model also spoke in turn of the kingdom of God of which David's kingdom was itself only a shadow. This kingdom of God is the one established through the gospel of Jesus Christ. The redemption from Egypt which, in its time, did not speak clearly of a redemption from sin, nevertheless pointed towards the gospel. The pattern of redemption seen in the history of Israel's exodus from Egypt found its fulfilment in Christ. The kingdom of priests are those who are redeemed from sin by the blood of Christ. Priests were "go-betweens". They went to God on behalf of the nation and to the nation on behalf of God. John describes all Christians as priests because they have access to God through the blood of Christ.

Notice how John ascribes glory and dominion to the one who suffered (Revelation 1:6). Here is the basis of the theme of the whole book. Here is the Lamb and the Lion. The Christ who suffered is now the ruling Lord. It is inevitable that all things must be made subject to him, and so his second coming in glory is a certainty. Until that time he conquers and rules through the message of his suffering. The godless do not know that their present rebellion against Christ will be turned to his glory because of his suffering. The Lamb will reveal his Lion-like qualities when he comes to judge the world. Then those whose rebellion has pierced the Lamb will be confounded (Revelation 1:7).

I must stress again the relationship that John has so quickly established between the first and second comings of Christ. The second coming is the unveiling of the Lamb to reveal the Lion. The two are one, and there is a basic sense in which the two comings of Christ are one. God alone knows how many years separate these two great events but, notwithstanding the passing of a long period of time, we must hold the two in the closest conjunction. It is the separating of the significance of these two events which has led to many of the wild interpretations of Revelation by prophetic specialists.

The same perspective is to be found in the vision of the glorified Christ in Revelation 1:12-16. John is overwhelmed by the majesty of this figure, the description of whom defies any adequate visual reproduction. When he says, "I fell at his feet as though dead" (verse 17), we can only suppose that John was filled with the realization of the enormous gulf that separated himself as a sinful being from the holy glory of the reigning Christ. He was like Isaiah brought by a vision of God's glory to cry "woe" in despair at his own sinfulness (Isaiah 6:5). He was like Job driven to realize his unworthiness before the Lord of the universe (Job 42:1-6). He was like Peter who, through an experience of catching fish, glimpsed for a moment the power of Christ and in panic cried, "Go away from me, Lord; I am a sinful man!" (Luke 5:1-8).

But John is comforted and restored with the message that this vision splendid is none other than the dying and rising Saviour (verse 18). John can stand before the Lion for he has been justified by the Lamb!

The letters to the churches are instructive in this regard (Revelation 2 and 3). John's view of Christian existence set out in these letters does not differ from that of Paul or Peter in their letters. All problems, heresies and deviations from the true course of Christian living which occupy the writers of the New Testament Epistles derive from the same basic problem: a failure to bring the gospel to bear on this or that aspect of life. Consequently there is only one remedy that can ever be prescribed and that is the gospel. This assertion may surprise many, for Christian living or the general question of sanctification (holiness) is so frequently dealt with in Christian teaching and preaching as if the gospel were only the means of beginning the Christian life, and not also the means of continuing it. The New Testament, however, teaches that it is the life, death and resurrection of Jesus Christ which constitute the meaning, motive and power for Christian living.[5]

Thus we find that the seven letters in Revelation contain the same perspective even though they use more of the symbolism and images of the Old Testament than either Paul or Peter. We may summarize the diagnoses thus:

1. The Ephesians have abandoned their first love. The gospel no longer grips and motivates them as it used to do (Revelation 2:4).
2. The Smyrnans are commended for their faithfulness and urged to persevere (Revelation 2:9-10).
3. The Church at Pergamum has allowed false teaching to enter. The gospel is compromised and those responsible invite retribution (Revelation 2:14-16).
4. The Thyatirans are in a similar position because of a false prophetess in their midst (Revelation 2:20).
5. In the church at Sardis love for the gospel has grown cold. The summons is to "remember what you have received and heard." Happily there are some who have not "soiled their clothes". These continue in faith in the Son of God by whose blood they are cleansed (Revelation 3:3-4).
6. The Philadelphians are commended for faithfulness in adversity (Revelation 3:8,10).
7. The Laodiceans have lost sight of the gospel and so have lost their fellowship with Christ. This same Christ waits to be readmitted: "If anyone hears my voice and opens

5. Herman Ridderbos states: That Paul's epistles give what is no longer the first announcement of this Gospel, but rather the further exposition and application of it, does not detract from the fact that this Gospel is the sole and constant subject of his epistles also; and that therefore, if one has to characterize their general content not only as kerygma [gospel proclamation], but also as doctrine [teaching] and paraenesis [exhortation], yet this doctrine, too, has no other object and this admonition no other starting point and ground than the fulfilling and redeeming activity of God in the advent of Christ. *Paul: An outline of His Theology* (Grand Rapids: Wm. B. Eerdmans, 1975, London, S.P.C.K., 1977), 47f. (Explanatory terms in brackets mine).

the door, I will go in and eat with him." The voice of
Christ is the word of the gospel and by this alone is fellowship with Christ re-established (Revelation 3:17,20).

In Revelation 4 and 5 we come to the vision of the Lion
who is the Lamb slain. I have already shown how this points
to the redeeming death of Christ as the key to the opening of
the scrolls containing the truth about the coming of the
kingdom of God. The opening of each seal in turn leads to
revelations of judgment. But the fifth seal (Revelation 6:9-11)
results in a vision of martyrs crying out for vindication:
"How long, Sovereign Lord, holy and true, until you judge
the inhabitants of the earth and avenge our blood?" The
purpose of this vision is not to tell us that the martyrs themselves are waiting for an answer, rather it is a means of
comfort to the living. Those who have died for the faith (and
those who will yet die), have not suffered in vain. They are
secure because they have the robe of Christ's righteousness.

When we turn to Revelation 11:15-19 there is a grand affirmation: "The kingdom of the world has become the kingdom
of our Lord and of his Christ, and he shall reign for ever and
ever." It could be argued from the exegesis of the text that it
refers primarily to the consummation at Christ's second
coming. However, it is interesting also to look at the context
of Revelation 11. The acclamation of the kingdom comes
when the seventh angel blows his trumpet. Between the sixth
trumpet (Revelation 9:13-21) and the seventh trumpet (Revelation 11:15-19) there is a passage which uses a number of Old
Testament ideas and events to describe the conflict between
the world and the agents of God's kingdom. In the face of
their prophesying and working of signs and wonders, the
world still does not repent. Rather, the beast from the pit
wars against them and kills them. But God raises them up and
takes them to heaven while a great destruction overcomes the
earth.

Then the seventh angel blows the trumpet and the reign of
Christ is announced. The elders respond with thanksgiving
that the Lord God has taken his great power and begun to
reign. The temple of God in heaven is opened and the ark of
the covenant seen. The conjunction of these two things is not
insignificant. The ark of the covenant can be seen because the

veil of the temple is removed. The kingdom of God is thus joined to the atoning death of Christ. The veilless temple in heaven recalls the tearing of the veil of the temple in Jerusalem at the moment Christ died. The way is open for all justified sinners to enter into the presence of God through the blood of Christ.

The first question then, is not "when" the kingdom of the world becomes the kingdom of Christ, but "how". This passage shows the ministry of the Old Testament prophets foreshadowing both the conflict between Christ and Satan, and the conflict between the church and the powers of darkness. The resurrection and the way of access to the ark of the covenant speak of the victory of Christ through the gospel event. Once we understand this we can sort out the "when". Clearly, there is a sense in which the victory of Christ is retrospective. The prophetic ministry of the Old Testament was in a real sense a gospel ministry. Moses turning the Nile to blood, Elijah stopping the rain, and every prophetic sign, all point to their fulfilment in the victory of Christ. Christ's miracles are a connecting link which show that the ministry of Christ is to fulfil the prophetic ministry by bringing in the kingdom. The resurrection of the martyrs and the opened temple are eloquent of the justification of the sinner.

Revelation 12 depicts the warfare in heaven between Michael the archangel and the dragon, who is Satan. The dragon is thrown down. Then John hears a voice saying:

> Now have come the salvation and the power and the kingdom of our God, and the authority of his Christ. For the accuser of our brothers, who accuses them before our God day and night, has been hurled down. They overcame him by the blood of the Lamb and by the word of their testimony; they did not love their lives so much as to shrink from death (Revelation 12:10-11).

At this point let us note that the casting down of Satan is seen as the event which signals two things: the coming of the authority and power of Christ and of the kingdom of God, and the salvation of God's people whereby they overcome. Satan is here designated the "accuser" of the brethren. The

name Satan is applied to the devil in the New Testament
because he functions as an accusing adversary. The Hebrew
word *satan* means adversary and is used in Job 1 to describe
the one who accuses Job before God.

Once again the apocalyptic style needs to be understood.
John is not concerned so much with a sequence of events as
with the dimensions of salvation. The spatial and temporal
sequences of this word picture are not to be pressed into a
literal description of the coming of the kingdom. Thus the
warfare is described first as waged by Michael against Satan.
The outcome, however, is that the brethren conquer Satan by
the blood of the Lamb. John is describing the gospel event.
The fact that the accuser is silenced means that the sinner is
declared by the judge to be "not guilty". He is justified.

The brethren also are said to overcome by the word of their
testimony for, says John, "they loved not their lives even
unto death". Testimony in the New Testament means a
witness to the person and work of Christ, that is, to the
gospel. The frequent reference to martyrs (or "witnesses") in
Revelation does not operate so as to exclude all non-martyrs.
John uses martyrdom to describe those who actually die for
the faith, and also those who "love not their lives", and thus
persevere to the end in the service of the gospel. What we
should recognize is that the New Testament does not use the
word testimony to describe the kind of "ego-trip" that some
Christians practise by parading themselves as living miracles.
Testimony is to the Christ of the gospel and to what he did
for us in his life and death.

Thus far it is apparent that the historic gospel is represented in many ways and by various images within the Book of
Revelation. My only reason for treating this matter by a
survey of Revelation chapter by chapter, is that I find it is so
often the forgotton dimension. I am not arguing for the
presence of references in Revelation to the historic gospel. I
doubt if any would disagree with that. Rather, I am arguing
that the Book of Revelation is about the gospel. The gospel is
its central theme. Above all it is speaking of the coming of the
kingdom of God through the victory of Christ at Calvary.
The kingdom of God means that the people of God are cleansed and accepted. They are justified by grace as a gift.

Perhaps no image is so pregnant with the theme of the justification of the sinner as that of Christ "the Lamb". For the Lamb is the Lamb only because he is the Lamb who was slain. This title is used in Revelation some 28 times. If only to complete our survey, we may observe the references to the Lamb in the remainder of the book. Revelation 14:1-5 shows the Lamb in Mount Zion with the 144,000 who sing a new song. They are described as chaste followers of the Lamb. In Revelation 15:2-4 John describes those who conquered the beast singing "the song of Moses and the song of the Lamb". The "new song" is a song of redemption (see Psalms 96:1; 98:1; 144:9f) and the song of Moses is a song of the Lord's victory as he redeems Israel from Egypt (see Exodus 15). The two passages are very similar: the redeemed praise God for his marvellous deeds by which they are saved. The song of Moses is the song of the Lamb. The exodus from Egypt is the shadow of the gospel.

Some of the more controversial texts relating to the Lamb occur in Revelation 20. I will delay discussion of them until I have laid the foundation for understanding that chapter. Notwithstanding that omission at this juncture, I propose that enough has been said to show that the gospel is at least a major theme of Revelation. As we proceed, the gospel will emerge as *the* controlling theme of the book.

The Literary Structure of Revelation
(See Figure 2, page 57)

It is time now to observe something of the basic literary structure of Revelation. It is not difficult to see that Revelation is more than a collection of disconnected visions and other material. How the contents are organically related will be discussed in a later chapter. For the moment I will suggest only a broad outline of the relation of the parts. Even a cursory look at the way different commentators handle the structure of Revelation will reveal considerable differences of opinion. This analysis is put forward as one possibility. It is not crucial to the understanding of the book, but rather proposed as an aid to the perception of an overall unity in design.

The Book of Revelation consists of six groups of mainly apocalyptic visions, preceded by a group of letters and followed by a climactic vision of the consummated kingdom. Austin Farrer suggests that the structure is sabbatical[6]. That is, there are six groups of seven followed by a final sabbath. Theologically, this is appealing because the New Jerusalem of Revelation 21-22 corresponds with the "sabbath rest of the people of God" (Hebrews 4:9-11). Other commentators do not find some of the groups of visions so easily divisible by seven, and this should prompt caution against being too quick to arrive at a neat and tidy analysis. However, it is difficult to deny that these groups exist and that they are mostly interspersed with sections which frequently describe a hymnic response to the visionary material. These sections act as interludes to connect the consecutive groups of visions.

Another connecting feature of these groups is that the second, third, and fourth of them delay the seventh part of their action until after the interlude. The seventh vision of the group then becomes the new group of seven. Thus, for example, the series of seven seals (Revelation 6) actually goes as far as the sixth seal. Then there is an interlude (Revelation 7), after which the seventh seal is opened (Revelation 8:1). What follows is not another act of judgment such as those that issued from the breaking of the first six seals. Instead John sees a new seven, this time the seven angels with trumpets. After a short introductory vision the angels proceed to blow the trumpets in turn (Revelation 8-9). Again we are taken only to the sixth trumpet before there is an interlude (Revelation 10-11). When the seventh trumpet is blown a new group of visions follows (Revelation 12-14). There is a difference of scholarly opinion as to the exact significance of this structure, but it cannot be doubted that it establishes a structural unity for the Book. The overall pattern may be represented as in Figure 2. Other questions of relationship, such as whether the groups are intended to be parallel or consecutive, must remain until we have further examined the intention of the book, and the method of carrying it out.

6. Op. cit.

Summary

The gospel is the historic event of the life, death and resurrection of Jesus Christ for us. Justification is the formal or doctrinal term used to refer to the principal significance of the gospel for the believing sinner. In Revelation John uses a variety of ways to present this gospel of our justification as the heart and soul of the Christian message. In the context of the sufferings of the Christians to whom he writes, John presents a message which is as relevant today as it was then: the Christian's comfort in adversity, his corrective in error, his motive for holiness, is the gospel and only the gospel.

THESIS
The doctrine of justification is basic to the message of Revelation and is woven throughout the book.

Figure 2

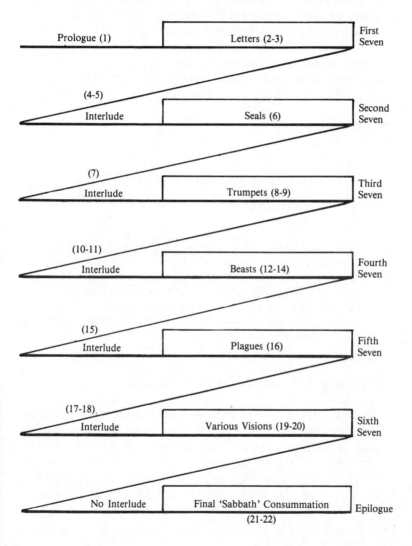

THE STRUCTURE OF
THE BOOK OF REVELATION

Chapters are shown in brackets

Prologue (1) | Letters (2-3) | First Seven

(4-5) Interlude | Seals (6) | Second Seven

(7) Interlude | Trumpets (8-9) | Third Seven

(10-11) Interlude | Beasts (12-14) | Fourth Seven

(15) Interlude | Plagues (16) | Fifth Seven

(17-18) Interlude | Various Visions (19-20) | Sixth Seven

No Interlude | Final 'Sabbath' Consummation (21-22) | Epilogue

4

'The great day of God Almighty'
Biblical Perspectives on the End of the World

Then I saw three evil spirits that looked like frogs;
they came out of the mouth of the dragon, out of the
mouth of the beast and out of the mouth of the false
prophet. They are spirits of demons performing miraculous signs, and they go out to the kings of the whole
world, to gather them for the battle on the great day of
God Almighty (Revelation 16:13-14).

The day of the Lord in the Old Testament

It would be surprising indeed if an author so heavily dependent, as John is, upon the Old Testament did not at some
stage introduce the notion of the day of the Lord to describe
the climax of God's war against evil. John makes specific
mention of the day of God several times.[1] The emphasis may
differ in these, but their relation to the saving action of God

1. eg. Revelation 1:10, the Lord's day; 6:17, the great day of their wrath;
16:14; 18:8, in one day.

can be confidently affirmed. The Old Testament establishes both the variety of emphasis and the ultimate significance of this use of *day*.

The day of the Lord is the day of his victory. It is the day on which the salvation of God is revealed and effected for all the people of God. On the other hand it is a day of wrath for all those who maintain their rebellious opposition to the kingdom of God. The actual phrase, "the day of the Lord", is sometimes varied or shortened to "that day", "coming days", or "those days". The occurrences which give us the clearest indication of meaning are in the prophets.[2] The earliest of these references is probably that of Amos who prophesied in the northern kingdom of Israel during the mid-eighth century B.C.

> Woe to you who long
>   for the day of the Lord!
> Why do you long for the day of the Lord?
> That day will be darkness, not light (Amos 5:18).

It seems that the phrase "day of the Lord" was known to the contemporaries of Amos and that it signified the expectation of a great benefit which would come by the hand of the Lord. This oracle (Amos 5:18-27) rejects such optimism because the formal worship of God by the Israelites was only a cloak for idolatry. They could thus anticipate only wrath:

> Therefore I will send you into exile beyond Damascus,
> says the Lord, whose name is God Almighty (Amos 5:27).

Zephaniah, who prophesized in the seventh century B.C., used the "day of the Lord" in the same way. It was to be a day of the wrath of God visited upon those who have broken the convenant of God (Zephaniah 1:7-18). Zephaniah resorts

2. Isaiah 2:12; 13:6,9; 22:5; 34:8; Jeremiah 46:10; Ezekiel 7:10; 13:5; 30:3; Joel 1:15; 2:1, 11, 31; 3:14; Amos 5:18-20; Zephaniah 1:7-8, 14-18; Zechariah 14:1.
   The meaning of the day of the Lord in the prophets is discussed in G. von Rad, *Old Testament Theology* (Edinburgh: Oliver and Boyd, 1965) Vol II, pp 119-125.

to the imagery of warfare and brings his oracle to a crescendo
of universal destruction:

> Neither their silver nor their gold
> will be able to save them
>   on the day of the Lord's wrath.
> In the fire of his jealousy
>   the whole world will be consumed,
> for he will make a sudden end
>   of all who live in the earth (Zephaniah 1:18).

Isaiah, the eighth-century prophet, is also familiar with the
wrath of the day of the Lord:

> The Lord Almighty has a day in store
> for all the proud and lofty,
> for all that is exalted
>   (and they will be humbled).
> The Lord alone will be exalted in that day,
> and the idols will totally disappear.
>
> Men will flee to caves in the rocks
> and to holes in the ground
> from the dread of the Lord
>   and the splendour of his majesty,
> when he rises to shake the earth (Isaiah 2:12, 17b-19).
>
> For the Lord has a day of vengeance,
> a year of retribution, to
>   uphold Zion's cause (Isaiah 34:8).
>
> See, the day of the Lord is coming
>   —a cruel day, with wrath
>   and fierce anger—
> to make the land desolate
>   and to destroy the sinners within it.
>
> The stars of the heaven and their constellations
> will not show their light.
> The rising sun will be darkened
>   and the moon will not give
>   its light (Isaiah 13:9-10).

In this latter passage one can easily see the imagery which is used also by Joel:

> I will show wonders in the heavens and on the earth,
> blood and fire and billows of smoke.
>
> The sun will be turned to darkness
>   and the moon to blood
> before the coming of the great
>   and dreadful day of the Lord (Joel 2:30-31).

The day of the Lord, then, is the day of his wrath against his enemies, the day of judgment. But it is also the day of the salvation of his people. That is why the ritual-loving but hypocritical Israelites anticipated it with optimism, and why Amos had to disabuse their minds with a warning of judgment. For those who truly wait for God there is a firm cause for optimism. Joel's prophecy, though similar to Isaiah's, is not concerned with wrath. The signs in the heavens are the accompaniments of blessing and salvation. The spirit of God will be poured out on the people (Joel 2:28) and everyone who calls on the name of the Lord will be saved (verse 32).

Gerhard von Rad has proposed that the idea of the day of the Lord emerged from the historical experience of Israel in the exodus from Egypt and the conquest of Canaan.[3] This is the day of the Lord's intervention as the divine warrior:

> The Lord is a warrior;
>   the Lord is his name.
> Pharaoh's chariots and his army
> he has hurled into the sea (Exodus 15:3-4).

The defeat of the haters of God's kingdom is the occasion of the salvation of the faithful:

> The Lord is my strength and my song;
> He has become my salvation.
> He is my God, and I will praise Him (Exodus 15:2).

---

3. loc. cit.

This means that the kingdom of God has come, for his enemies are destroyed and his people redeemed:

> You will bring them in and plant them
> on the mountain of your inheritance—
> the place, O Lord, you made for your dwelling,
> the sanctuary, O Lord, your hands established.
> The Lord will reign for ever and ever (Exodus 15:17-18).

The day of the Lord means the coming of the kingdom of God, which brings judgment to God's enemies and salvation to his people. The exodus was certainly a pattern-making event in Israel's history which established the concept of the redemptive act of God. It spoke of the release of the Israelites from a godless captivity that negated all that the covenant promises had made over to the chosen people. It spoke of the miraculous event by which an imprisoned people were set free to serve the living God. It marked the point at which it became possible for the descendants of Abraham to enter the land of their inheritance.

When this historical experience of Israel, which patterned salvation, reached its climax in the kingdom of David and Solomon, the rot set in. As the strength and faithfulness of Israel declined and the whole fabric which pre-figured the kingdom of God crumbled and fell apart, the truth of the kingdom was given to the prophetic word of revelation. The oracles that we have considered concerning the day of the Lord belong to this period of decline. The prophets continued the process of revelation about the kingdom of God by injecting into the actual decline of Israel's glory the word of judgment and of hope. They depicted a devastating act of God's wrath on all who broke the covenant with God, along with all the godless nations, and they depicted beyond tragedy the renewed nation of Israel resurrected in glory.

The prophets use many and varied images to describe the new age beyond the final act of God to judge and to save. However, the prophetic words of hope all build upon the past history of Israel. The model of an Israelite monarchy centring upon the Davidic prince ruling at the temple of Jerusalem becomes the essential concept which is glorified and perfected in the futuristic projection of the kingdom of God.[4] Both the history of Israel and the prophetic view of the kingdom testify to the inseparability of the elements of judgment and salvation. The salvation of the people of God cannot be achieved without judgment upon all the powers of darkness which resist God's kingdom. But this visitation of wrath upon the spiritual powers of darkness, inevitably gathers up and includes all those human beings who have sided with darkness by their wilful opposition to God. The prophets had to make the unacceptable point that many of the people of the covenant had put themselves into that reprobate category by their evil covenant-breaking ways.

One characteristic of the prophetic expression is important for this discussion. The prophets were not bound, as we of the twentieth century so often are, by strict attention to chronology and sequence. They were quite happy to look at the same event now from this point of view, now from that. Furthermore, events which subsequently proved themselves to be distinct in time, were easily spoken of as if this distinction were unimportant. Let us be clear about this. The prophets did not sit loosely to the idea of history. They were immersed in time and history. But they did not view time and history from the same stand-point as a modern scientific historian.

Wherein lay the difference between the prophetic and the modern approach to time and history? Well, for one thing the prophets were convinced that all history was in the hand of God. Chronological sequences and cause-effect considerations were all subsumed under the sovereign will of God. Nor was this a fatalistic view of deity. Rather it was a covenantal view. Jehovah the God of Israel had revealed himself as the creator and Lord of history, but also as the redeemer of Israel. Time and history took their meaning from these facts. Nothing in history had meaning apart from God and his self-revealing, redemptive acts. It was the redemptive quality of the time rather than the quantity of the time which concerned

4. The restoration prophecies which depict the coming kingdom in terms of a glorified recapitulation of the old Israelite monarchy include: Isaiah 2:1-4; 4:2-6; 9:6-7; 52:1-12; 60:1-22; 61:1-7; 65:17-25; Jeremiah 23:1-8; 31:1-40; Ezekiel 34-48.

them most.[5] In this the prophets laid the foundation for the
New Testament view of history which likewise treated it very
seriously but subjected the quantitative aspect to the qualitative. It did this by interpreting history in the light of the
gospel.

In the prophets of the Old Testament we see concern con-
centrated upon the redemptive characteristics of the historical
events (whether past or future history). So the "day of the
Lord" emerged from the past history of the Lord's warfare
against his enemies in the exodus from Egypt and the conquest of Canaan. The prophets, when they speak of a future
manifestation of the wrath of God, may describe it as local
(e.g. a specific imminent historic catastrophe such as Israel
being exiled), or as universal (a total destruction of all the
enemies of God), or as cosmic (a complete dismantling of the
created order). All of these manifestations can be seen as
belonging to the "day of the Lord". In their view of salvation the prophets may describe it as an actual and predicted
return of Jewish exiles to their land after a certain number of
years (e.g. Jeremiah's prediction that 70 years would see a
return from Babylon), or as an unspecified future event when
all the true covenant people would be restored from whatever
land they had been dispersed to, or as a cosmic renovation of
all creation. Again all these possibilities fit the category of the
"day of the Lord".

What we should note is this: though the prophets gave expression to these different dimensions of both judgment and
salvation, they really did not concern themselves with the
distinctions between them as such, nor with how they were
related in actual time and history. It was enough that the day
of the Lord was coming. The reality of God's wrath and of
his redeeming love had been seen in times past and it would
be seen again in the future. As the prophets looked to the
future from their standpoint in the midst of the historical
failure of Israel to be the redeemed people of God, they saw
the day of the Lord as the final act. Beyond that there could

5. By no means may we allow these characteristics of prophetic thinking to
   support the thoroughly unbiblical views which dismiss historical fact as
   irrelevant. The prophets were not indifferent to history. However, they
   were not governed by twentieth century views of history.

be no failure as in the past, but only the everlasting glory of God's kingdom. The various dimensions of the coming of the kingdom (local, world-wide and cosmic) all belonged without differentiation to the one great day of the Lord that was coming. (See Fig. 3 on p.66.)

The apocalyptic view of the day of the Lord has one obvious difference from the prophetic view. Since it is not realistic to separate the prophetic and apocalyptic views of the future (they overlap in many respects), we should say that the distinction is one of emphasis as well as of literary idiom. It is generally accepted that the apocalyptic idiom gives much sharper definition to the transition from the old age to the new age of the kingdom of God. Gone is the prophetic appeal to repentance that will avert the impending judgment. Gone also is the distinctly Israelite national emphasis. Instead the apocalyptists tend to depict the inevitable and unavoidable progress of the present evil age to the point where God says, "No more!" Then in a catastrophic intervention of God the old is destroyed and the new age emerges. It is not so much the salvation of Israel that is presented, though that is there too, but the transformation of all creation.

When we have allowed for the differences in emphasis in prophetic and apocalyptic writing, we are still left with an important common feature which may be said to characterize the Old Testament view of history and the end of the age. Despite the fact that the prophets acknowledge the respective nature of redemptive acts and judgment (e.g. in history of Israel's exodus and conquest of the land, in the exile and return from Babylon, and in the final day of the Lord), the future day of the Lord is spoken of in a way which does not concern itself with how the local, universal and cosmic elements are related in time. The effect is an undifferentiated view of the end. The day of the Lord means the salvation of the people of God and the judgment of his enemies.

The apocalyptic emphasis, then, did not serve to displace or even drastically to qualify, the prophetic view of the day of the Lord. Rather it served only to sharpen certain aspects already present in prophetic preaching. Together the prophetic and apocalyptic views painted a picture of the linear succession of the two ages. This present age comes to an end at the point where the redemptive and judging acts of God reach their climax and final expression on the day of the Lord. At that point, and without further ado, the new age of the kingdom of God is revealed. A lot happens on the "day". Not only are the enemies of God finally put down, but Israel —the true believing Israel—is restored to the promised land. Jerusalem and the temple are re-built and the Davidic rule re-inaugurated. Then the gentiles, who are to be included, come running, seeking to be accepted because they have seen the glory of God revealed in the redemption of Israel (Isaiah 2:1-4; Zechariah 8:20-23). That day is the day on which the Spirit of God is poured out on people. It is a day in which salvation can still come to all who call on the name of the Lord (Joel 2:28-32). Quantitatively it is difficult to define this day, but qualitatively it is the day of salvation.

Figure 3

THE TWO AGES IN THE
OLD TESTAMENT

Prophetic Emphasis

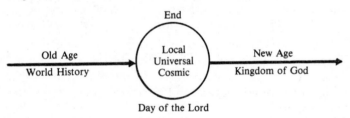

Apocalyptic Emphasis

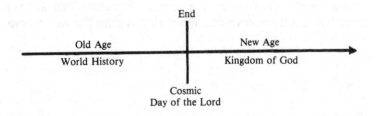

The Day of the Lord in the New Testament

Reflect on the fact that Old Testament history ended without the predicted day of the Lord having come. Then for nearly four hundred years the Jewish people went through successive dominations of their land and threats to their religion and culture. Finally, after the Persian and Greek empires had come and gone in turn, the land of the Jews became a small oppressed province of the Roman Empire. In the midst of this unpromising experience an event of great moment took place. A child, Jesus, was born and grew up, eventually to be recognized by a small group of people as the promised Messiah who would bring in the kingdom of God.

By signs and wonders, by word and deed, he began to impress upon his followers that he was truly God's Messiah. But for most of them this could mean only one thing: the day of the Lord was about to break. The wrath of God would come upon covenant breakers, the godless, and in particular, on the cruel and overbearing power of Rome. Then suddenly Jesus began to tell them that *he* was going to Jerusalem to die. "Not so!" said Peter, who must then suffer the stinging rebuke, "Get behind me Satan." Inexorably the events moved to their climax and the messianic prince of David, instead of ascending a golden throne, was nailed to a cross. The disciples' hopes were dashed; it was not the day of the Lord after all! The body of the leader was hurriedly put away before the sabbath began, and his followers withdrew to lick their wounds.

The following Sunday morning the incomprehensible happened: the crucified Master rose from the dead and showed himself alive to his friends. Suddenly their hopes were revived. Perhaps the kingdom of God would appear at this time after all. They begin to anticipate the glorious transition from being a tiny downtrodden nation within the vast Roman Empire, to being the shining glory of God, the centre of the earth and the envy of all nations. Gone would be the corrupt and the cruel Edomite kingship of the Herodians, and in its place would be the glory of the rule of the Davidic prince. Justice and peace would flow forth from the new Zion and the earth would become once more like the garden of Eden.

When the risen Jesus had been with the disciples for some days without the appearance of the kingdom, there was understandably some discussion amongst them about it. Finally, one day when they were together with Jesus, the question was put: "Lord, are you at this time going to restore the kingdom to Israel?" (Acts 1:6). What had happened to that "day of the Lord" of which the Old Testament spoke so graphically? So they were still hard of hearing and obtuse in their minds! On the day he rose, Jesus had rebuked two of them for not believing that other less palatable message of the prophets—that the Christ had to suffer before entering his glory (Luke 24:26). But now they accepted the suffering aspect, for it had been branded on their minds by the events of Good Friday. Could they not now expect to see Jesus enthroned as the Prince of Peace on the throne of David? "Lord, are you at this time going to restore the kingdom to Israel?"

Jesus' answer is decisive: "It is not for you to know the times or dates the Father has set by his own authority. But you will receive power when the Holy Spirit comes upon you; and you will be my witnesses in Jerusalem, and in all Judea and Samaria, and to the ends of the earth" (Acts 1:7-8). Some argue that because Jesus said, "It is not for you to know the times", he implied that the expectation of the disciples as to the nature of the kingdom and its coming was correct. Only their impatient desire to know "when" was misplaced. On this view the promise of the Spirit is diversionary rather than integral to the answer to the question. We should then expect that the future teaching of the apostles would clearly distinguish the two things—the coming of the kingdom in exactly the terms (if that were possible) of the Old Testament prophets, and the Spirit-filled preaching of the gospel as some kind of interim activity until the kingdom comes. In fact this is *not* what happened.

First, we note that once the Spirit was given at Pentecost, the question about the kingdom ceased to have relevance, for the answer was known. The apostles preached the gospel to the Jews for what it was, the fulfilment of all the hopes of Israel, all the promises of the prophets. Christ had indeed entered his glory through his resurrection and ascension. No

wonder that Christians came to refer to the day of resurrection, the first day of the week, as the day of the Lord.

Secondly, when the Spirit was given, Peter declared that
this was in fulfilment of Joel's prophecy of the day of the
Lord (Acts 2:15-21). It does not worry him that Joel also
referred to the signs such as the darkening of the sun and
reddening of the moon. He points to Joel's beautiful
assurance that "everyone who calls on the name of the Lord
will be saved". Then without further ado he preaches the
gospel of Christ and calls upon his hearers to repent and be
baptized. Truly this is the day of the Lord and the Davidic
prince reigns gloriously in Zion:

> But he (David) was a prophet and knew that God had
> promised to him on oath that he would place one of his
> descendants on his throne. Seeing what was ahead, he
> spoke of the resurrection of the Christ (Acts 2:30-31).

Compare these words with Paul's in his first sermon at
Antioch:

> We tell you the good news: What God promised our
> fathers he has fulfilled for us, their children, by raising
> up Jesus (Acts 13:32-33).

We find no deviation from this conviction in the rest of the
New Testament. With one voice the authors proclaim the
death and resurrection of Jesus as the point at which all the
promises of God reach their fulfilment. This is truly the day
of the Lord.

Thirdly, we note that along with the preaching of the gospel
there is an assurance that Christ not only reigns now, but that
he will return to manifest his kingship to all principalities and
powers. It is the giving of the Spirit coupled with the ascension
of Jesus that structures the fulfilment of the day of the Lord
in the New Testament. The Spirit's task is to illuminate the
believers with the truth of the gospel so that they can preach it
down through the ages. The Spirit makes real to mankind the
meaning of the gospel as the means which God uses to establish the kingdom. Since Christ ascended before manifesting
the glory of his kingdom, the Holy Spirit comes to enable the

church to preach the gospel. It is by this means alone that the kingdom comes in the world, but by the gospel the kingdom *does* come. Finally Christ "will appear a second time, not to bear sin, but to bring salvation to those who are waiting for him" (Hebrews 9:28).

In this brief description we see that the Holy Spirit applied the gospel to the minds of the apostles in such a way as to demand a qualification of the Old Testament perspective. The seeds of this qualification were already there in the Old Testament, not just in the motif of the suffering servant of which Jesus reminded the two disciples (Luke 24:26), but in the very structure of revealed truth. Israel had already received a clue in the fact that salvation was something they looked back on (Passover and Exodus), salvation was an on-going reality of daily life, and salvation was an expectation for the future (day of the Lord). It was partly their obtuseness and partly their baldly literal approach to the promises which made them reduce the day of the Lord to a purely future undifferentiated event.

What then, was the effect of the gospel as the Holy Spirit made it plain to the apostles' minds? The main adjustment was that they saw that the day of the Lord covered the past, the present and the future. In the past the day of the Lord was the decisive historic event of the life, death and resurrection of Jesus. He embodied in his person the perfection of all the covenant relationships between God and man. In that sense he was the kingdom of God come FOR US. The day of the Lord came as the wrath of God was poured out upon our substitute when he hung on the cross. The day of the Lord came as the people of God rose from the grave in the person of their substitute and ascended to sit with him at the right hand of God (Romans 6:1-10; Ephesians 2:4-6; Colossians 3:1-3). (See Fig. 4 on p.71.)

Because of this decisive work of God in Christ for our justification the Spirit is given. The coming of the Spirit, a continuous coming since Pentecost, is the coming of the day of the Lord. The Spirit comes because of the merits of Christ on our behalf (Acts 2:33). Through the preaching of the gospel the Holy Spirit makes the kingdom real to all who believe. The once for all end of the age in the historic Jesus Christ is so applied to the believer that by faith he is made a partaker of it *in Christ.* But in so doing the Spirit brings the day of the Lord into the present. Sanctification is the end of the age being applied to our existence.

Finally the end will be openly manifest. It will no longer be something that only believers acknowledge by faith. It will be the irresistible and undeniable sense- experience of all. While

Figure 4

TWO PERSPECTIVES ON THE END

Old Testament Perspective:
ONE MANIFESTATION OF THE END

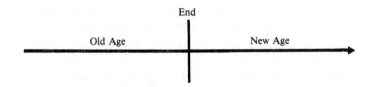

New Testament Perspective:
THREE MANIFESTATIONS OF THE END

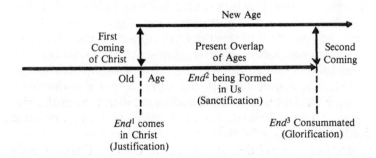

This diagram is based on that of Geerhardus Vos, The Pauline Eschatology *(Grand Rapids: Wm. B. Eerdmans Publishing Company, 1972), p.38 and is used by permission.*

Christ is known through the preaching of the gospel as the slain Lamb, only the gift of the Spirit to the elect will awaken faith in the reality that the Lamb has now, at this very moment, the glory of the Lion at the right hand of God. But, when Christ returns in glory to judge, though he will eternally be the Lamb, he will be revealed in the glory of the Lion both to judge, and to consummate our salvation.

The New Testament gospel thus restructures the coming of the kingdom in a way that it is vital for us to grasp. There is in effect an overlap of the two ages from the first coming to the second coming of Christ. This creates the Lamb-Lion tension which characterizes Christian existence in this period between the two comings. It is the tension between being in the world (as far as empirical experience goes), but not of it. It is the tension between being of the kingdom, but not in it (as far as empirical experience goes). As the Lamb suffered until the glory of his kingdom was bestowed at his resurrection and ascension, so the body of Christ must suffer until we likewise are (actually in ourselves) raised and transformed into the glory of Christ's image.

It is a thesis of this book that John, in Revelation, has made considerable use of prophetic and apocalyptic material in which the typical and traditional Old Testament perspective of the *end* or the day of the Lord is maintained. The New Testament perspective is provided by the nature of the gospel which, as we have seen, everywhere pervades the book. Thus, unless we are aware of this necessary qualification of the Old Testament perspective by the gospel we shall be likely to misread the nature of the visions of Revelation. It is my considered opinion that this very basic error of not allowing John to use Old Testament forms—prophetic oracles and apocalyptic visions—without modification is one cause of much prophetic speculation about the Book of Revelation today. It is regrettably true that much Christian literature and preaching has lost the essential ingredient of a sound method of interpretation. It has allowed the gospel to be demoted into something less than the preeminent and central characteristic which interprets the whole meaning of the Bible. I shall endeavour to apply this gospel-centred interpretation of the Book of Revelation.

Summary

The Old Testament idea of the day of the Lord is central to the view of the end of the world that is set forth in the prophetic and apocalyptic writings. The old age passes away and the terrible day of God introduces the new age of Israel's glory. Related to this concept is the theme of God the divine warrior who fights for his people, judging his enemies and bringing salvation to his chosen. The New Testament proclaims that the day of the Lord has come with Jesus Christ who fulfils all prophetic promise. The resurrection and ascension of Jesus, coupled with Pentecost, show that the gospel modifies the Old Testament perspective in that the old and the new ages are seen to overlap for a time. John uses Old Testament literary forms, in particular the apocalyptic vision, largely without modification. Revelation thus contains many sections which speak of the day of the Lord in Old Testament terms.

THESIS

The Old Testament perspective of the day of the Lord, which is contained in John's apocalyptic visions, is modified by the gospel. The linear succession of the ages becomes the overlap of the ages between the first and second comings of Christ.

5

'To him who overcomes'

The Letters to the Seven Churches

Yet I hold this against you: You have forsaken your
first love. Remember the height from which you have
fallen! Repent and do the things you did at first. If you
do not repent, I will come to you and remove your
lampstand from its place. But you have this in your
favour: You hate the practices of the Nicolaitans, which
I also hate.

He who has an ear, let him hear what the Spirit says
to the churches. To him who overcomes I will give the
right to eat from the tree of life, which is in the paradise
of God (Revelation 2:4-7).

The Function of the Seven Letters

The letters to the seven churches in Revelation 2-3 are in
danger of being separated from the rest of the book. The
reason is not hard to find. Of all the several parts of Revelation, these seven short letters provide fewest difficulties and
stand most easily on their own. The fact that they are written
as letters, and deal with pastoral problems in real congrega-

tions of Christian people, puts them in the same general category as all the other New Testament epistles. Despite some
distinct characteristics which mark them out from the other
epistles, they employ a familiar technique of exhortation.
There are a number of peripheral questions of interest which
I prefer to leave to the many commentators on Revelation
because I do not think the answers will greatly affect our
understanding of the Book. For example: what is John's
source of information about these churches and what is his
relationship to them which enabled him to write the way he
does?

It is possible that John's address to seven churches in Revelation 1:4—"John to the seven churches that are in Asia ..."
—is intended as a preface only to the section ending with the
letter to Laodicea. I do not think, however, that such is the
case. It would disrupt the unity of the book and obscure the
relationship between the seven letters and the rest of the
book. It is quite possible, in view of the repeated use of seven
that the seven churches are representative of the total number
of churches in western Asia Minor. In this case Revelation is
a kind of general epistle to all the persecuted and struggling
groups of Christians with which John could so easily identify
in his own suffering and exile.

In considering the function of the seven letters, then, we
must not forget the preliminary section in Chapter 1:4-20, for
it is this which is addressed to the seven churches. In Chapter
3 above I have dealt with the gospel content of this section. It
would suffice, therefore, to remark that Revelation 1:4-20 is
a beautifully constructed and vividly presented expression of
the gospel in relation to John personally and to the churches
generally. The frequent references to significant passages in
the Old Testament presentation of salvation history create a
richness in the theological overtones that is almost breath-
taking. In the space of five short verses (v.4-8), John has
summed up the doctrine of God, the doctrine of the person of
Christ, the doctrine of salvation and the doctrine of the end
things. As daunting as that sounds, we find that it is the
person of Jesus Christ which holds it all together in perfect
unity. Christ is the one who brings God's grace, and he it is
who bears witness to truth, who rises from the dead to rule

the kings of the earth. Christ it is who loves us and has saved us to become children of the kingdom and priests to God. And Christ, this dying-rising Christ, it is who will appear again in majesty.

This summary of the gospel in action then leads into John's affirmation that Jesus is Lord. In the same way as does Peter in the Pentecost sermon of Acts 2, or Paul in Philippians 2, John describes the exaltation of Christ as a sequel to the suffering servanthood of Jesus of Nazareth (Revelation 1:9-20). John's unique reference to "the Lord's day" in verse 10 is usually taken to mean that it was Sunday when he received these visions. If it can be sustained that the term was used to designate the first day of the week in John's time, it still does not detract from the distinct possibility that John makes reference to the day for its theological overtones rather than to pass on the trivial piece of information about what day of the week it was. In other words John would be referring to the fact that it is Sunday because the central matter is the day of salvation and judgment which has come in Jesus Christ, and of which Sunday as the day of resurrection, is now the perpetual memorial.

When John is prostrated by the vision of Christ's glory he is gently comforted with the words, "Fear not" (v.17). The similarity between this passage and the "assurance of salvation" that is sometimes pronounced by the Old Testament prophets is striking: e.g.

> Fear not, for I have redeemed you;
>   I have called you by name;
> You are mine. (Isaiah 43:1)

The force in the assurance of salvation lay in the reminder of what God had done to save his people. This is put simply and powerfully to John with the words, "I died, and behold I am alive forever and ever" (v.18). The gospel is thus summed up in the death and resurrection of the now reigning Christ.

Now we should observe that the words of Christ to John beginning in verse 17, lead on to the seven letters. There is no break. The vision of Christ in glory and the assurance of salvation are the preamble to the seven messages. These

messages are not given as the words of John to the churches
but rather as the verbatim messages of Christ which John is
told to pass on to the churches. They are the epistles of Jesus
Christ who holds the churches in his hand (Revelation 1:16,
20; 2:1). Each of the seven messages begins with some reference to the Christ portrayed in the preceding vision.[1] Furthermore, each of these references has a counterpart in the consummation of the kingdom described in Revelation 21 and
22. That which John has by revelation is that which belongs
to the whole church through what God has revealed in Jesus
Christ. Christ in glory continues to be known as the suffering
Christ in the gospel. But the things belonging to his present
glory are the treasures in heaven which the gospel procures
for us and secures for all who believe. What we now know
by faith will be the experience of our senses in the
consummation.

The seven messages, then, serve to remind us that the
drama of redemption has its on-going effects in the world.
The fact that Christ has conquered, but wills to extend his
conquest into the lives of men and women through the preaching of the gospel, puts the church in the midst of the
apocalyptic war. Furthermore, this warfare is not purely
external, for it is also within each individual as the old nature
struggles against the new, the flesh against the spirit. It would
be a grossly distorted perspective if we saw the spiritual
warfare as only outside of us. The seven messages translate
the cosmic and spiritual warfare into the present human
existence of the people of God. The struggle is hard and the
suffering great. But always the vision of Christ in glory stands
over every consideration of our human predicament. In the
gospel event he overcame decisively. As Oscar Cullmann puts
it, the decisive victory of Calvary and the resurrection has
determined once and for all the outcome.[2] The sanctifica-
tional struggle of the church may be likened to the mopping-
up operations. Without the seven messages the Book of
Revelation would lose that valuable point of contact with our
present human experience. It would seem remote and

1. 2:1 from 1:13,16; 2:8 from 1:17,18; 2:12 from 1:16; 2:18 from 1:14-15;
   3:1 from 1:4,16; 3:7 is the converse of 1:18; 3:14 from 1:5.
2. *Christ and Time* (London: S.C.M. Press, 1951).

detached from our struggle. Whereas Jewish apocalyptic had appeared in danger of losing the cutting edge of the prophetic demand to repentance and faithfulness to the covenant, John restores this emphasis before he moves on to the visions of heavenly reality.

As we look at the structure of these seven messages we see that there is a marked uniformity. We may summarize thus:[3]

1. Address to the angel of the church.
2. Description of the author, Christ.
3. Reference to works followed by praise or criticism.
4. Warning of consequences of faithlessness.
5. Exhortation to persevere.
6. Promise to all who overcome.

What may we learn from these clear emphases in the letters?

First, the Christ who addresses the churches is their risen Lord and Saviour who holds them in his hands. He has won for all his people the prizes which are given to those who persevere. He is not therefore a tyrannical Lord but a loving Lord who plans to share his kingdom with those for whom he has laid down his life in his own humiliation and servant-hood. The sovereignty of Christ is such that we cannot weaken it. The emphasis of apocalyptic was that none can thwart the purpose of God nor withstand his will. There are many mysteries attaching to the sovereign will of God, and in our conceited attempts to solve them we often fall into the terrible error of diluting divine sovereignty into something which is a grotesque counterfeit. The danger arises particularly when we want to appeal to human responsibility in Christian living. One hears preachers and teachers talking about God as if he were utterly dependent upon us for the success of his redemptive plan. God is said to be unable to carry out his purpose unless we first do something. God can't use us until we get rid of every known sin. God can't send us the gift of the Spirit until we totally commit ourselves to him. And so it goes on, with God being effectively reduced to the architect of a good idea, but being powerless to carry it out without our help!

---

3. There are some slight variations, especially in the warnings and exhortations.

Christ will have none of this in his revelation to John. The first three chapters of Revelation set forth the seeming paradox of the sovereignty of the Lord of the church and the human responsibility of his people. This has often been a problem to Christians. How can God be absolutely sovereign at the same time as man is absolutely responsible? Surely the one cancels out the other. The attempts to resolve the paradox by either diluting God's sovereignty or by curtailing man's responsibility are the attempts of the sinful mind of man to dictate the truth about God on the basis of human reason. The Christian mind is informed and renewed by the gospel, though even Christians go on bringing non-Christian ways of thinking to the problems of the Bible. The truth of the matter, as always, is in the gospel. The problem of sovereignty and responsibility is the problem of how a truly sovereign God can go on being truly sovereign while relating to truly responsible man. The gospel does not solve the problem in the sense of telling us *how* in a way that is able to be fully understood by the human mind. Rather it shows us that the mystery is characteristic of God himself. For in the gospel we see the incomprehensible has happened: true sovereign God and true responsible man have united in the one person Jesus Christ. In the history of the early church we can see how Christians grappled with this mystery. But every time they were tempted to solve the mystery either by reducing the deity of Christ to fit in logically with his humanity, or vice versa, the result was a destruction of the gospel itself. Orthodox Christianity learned to live with the mystery and indeed, to glory in it. Jesus Christ was true God in union with true man in such a way that neither nature was diminished by the other nor confused with it.[4]

The gospel thus points us to and confirms us in this perspective which is everywhere in the New Testament. Here in Revelation John depicts the glories of the reigning Christ who

4. At the Council of Chalcedon in 451 the church devised a formula for speaking about this mystery. In Christ there is true God and true man. There is a union of the two natures but no fusion. There is a distinction between them, but no separation. The church also came to realise that this "unity-distinction" way of speaking about Christ pointed also to the nature of God himself as three persons in one God.

holds the churches in his hands. His sovereignty is a reality now. But, as always, the sovereign Lord expresses his sovereignty, not by bypassing our minds and wills, but by working through them. To the mind which is uninformed by the gospel, this is a contradiction. Many Christians show that they have not brought the gospel to bear on their thinking when they reject, for example, the sovereign predestination of God as being incompatible with human responsibility. The union of God and man in Jesus Christ shows that this is not so. In fact, far from being incompatible, sovereignty and responsibility are shown to be the best of friends. Jesus Christ was the most perfect expression of humanity. He was the perfectly integrated personality, exhibiting all the virtues of humanity with none of the blemishes of sin. He may not have been conventional, and he often offended his enemies and sometimes even his friends. But he was the perfect pattern of God relating to humanity. He was the living interpretation of the doctrine of creation and of the nature of man as created in the image of God. He was and is true sovereign God and true responsible man.

Secondly, as we bring this perspective to bear on the seven messages of Revelation 2-3 we see the sovereign Lord addressing the churches which are made up of responsible people who are thus answerable for their actions. These letters clearly show that human effort and good works, and being held answerable for our works, are in no way incompatible with divine sovereignty. Furthermore, they are perfectly in harmony with the gospel doctrine of justification by faith alone on the basis of Christ's merits alone. Good works and rewards are part of New Testament teaching and they are not to be regarded as somehow contradicting justification as a free gift. The distinctive contribution of the seven messages in Revelation is to show that the good works of the people of God are part of the apocalyptic struggle between the reigning Christ and the powers of darkness. The accountability of Christians is thus highlighted. The significance of good works goes beyond mere kindness to one's neighbours and helping the missionary cause. The struggles of the local churches to live out the gospel, to resist the impact of non-christian values and ideas, and to stay true to the revelation of God in Jesus

Christ, are all part of the conquest of the world through the gospel. Behind the scenes the same conquest is being effected in the reign of Christ in heaven. In the world the church must be content to follow the example of the Lamb in his sufferings, but it is assured that the Lamb's sufferings are the key to the conquest of the Lion.

The Question of Rewards

Rewards in the New Testament, on first appearances, seem to contradict the teaching that Christians are justified by faith alone. Justification means that God accepts us for what Christ has done in our place. Since he has done the same for each and every believer, we would assume that each and every believer will receive the same inheritance in the kingdom of God. So where do rewards fit in? Are there going to be *A class* and *B class* mansions in heaven? In fact the problem is less pronounced in the seven letters than in some other parts of the New Testament as we shall see later on. But first let us consider the matter generally.[5]

To begin with, we note Calvin's argument that all good works must be regarded as God's gift and therefore cannot be the grounds of merit. It is the grace of God which produces good works in us. They are the fruit of the merits of Christ. This is not contrary to referring to them as the fruit of the Spirit since it is the merits of Christ that won for all God's people the gift of the Spirit. Now the outcome of this is the final glorification of the believer and his full inheritance of the "reward", the kingdom of God. The whole process of salvation, starting with God's election and call, involves our justification on the basis of Christ's merits, our sanctification through the Spirit (also on the basis of Christ's merits), and our final inheritance of glory.

5. The whole subject of works and rewards in relation to Justification is dealt with superbly by John Calvin, *Institutes of the Christian Religion* Book III, Chapters 14-18. Calvin is usually considered to be suited only for the advanced reader. He is however surprisingly simple and readable. An excellent basic treatment of this subject is given by Robert Horn, *Go Free!* (Downers Grove: Inter Varsity Press, 1976).

The sanctification of the Christian is, therefore, in one sense automatic. We cannot take hold of Christ by faith for our justification without the Holy Spirit. It is the same Holy Spirit that both enables the sinner to believe the gospel and also works in us his fruit of sanctification. In another sense sanctification is not automatic in that the Spirit works through our minds and wills. All the admonition and exhortation in the Bible is God's way of involving us in the sanctifying work of the Spirit. To be human is to be responsible. To be Christianly human is to respond with mind and will to the gospel with good works.

Paul's magnificent description of Christ, the suffering servant, becoming the reigning Lord (Philippians 2:6-11) is immediately followed by this exhortation, in which he points up the implication of the fact that "Jesus Christ is Lord":

> Therefore, my dear friends, as you have always obeyed—not only in my presence, but now much more in my absence—continue to work out your salvation with fear and trembling, for it is God who works in you to will and to act according to his good purpose (Philippians 2:12-13).

Here we see sovereignty and responsibility knit together in such a way that the outworking of salvation day by day—good works—is immediately the result of human effort, but ultimately the work of God in us.

Listen to Calvin:

> Why, then, are we justified by faith? Because by faith we grasp Christ's righteousness, by which alone we are reconciled to God. Yet we could not grasp this without at the same time grasping sanctification also. For he "is given unto us for righteousness, wisdom, sanctification, and redemption." Therefore Christ justifies no one whom he does not at the same time sanctify. These benefits are joined together by an everlasting and indissoluble bond, so that those whom he illumines by his wisdom, he redeems; those whom he redeems, he justifies; those whom he justifies, he sanctifies.

> Thus it is clear how true it is that we are justified not
> without works yet not through works, since in our
> sharing in Christ, which justifies us, sanctification is
> just as much included as righteousness (*Institutes*, III.
> 16.1).

Calvin goes on to indicate that reference to rewards does
not thereby imply that works are the cause of salvation. Yet
because of the intimate connection between them and the fact
that good works both follow justification and also precede
final glorification, the inheritance of the saints may be
spoken of as reward. In the final analysis there is no distinction between the inheritance, which is a gift of grace, and
reward. But since it is God's purpose to bring us to our
inheritance by way of the race of good works, the term
reward appropriately emphasizes our human responsibility in
this race. Again Calvin comments:

> The Lord rewards the works of believers with the
> same benefits as He had given them before they contem-
> plated any works, as He does not yet have any reason to
> benefit them except His own mercy (*Institutes*, III.
> 18.2).

Overcoming by Faith

Each of the seven letters of Revelation begins with an
ascription to Christ as the author and then begins, "I know
your works". In the case of Smyrna it is "I know your tribulation", and Pergamum, "I know where you dwell". Each
church receives a commendation, except Laodicea, but each
commendation, except that of Smyrna, is qualified by a
phrase like, "I have this against you". Each is exhorted
accordingly to repentance, endurance, or perseverance. Every
letter closes with a promise to "him who overcomes".
Although the performance of these churches is mostly referred to as works, the relationship of these works to faith in
Christ, or faithfulness to the word of the gospel, is everywhere apparent. Furthermore, faith which issues in good
works, in the face of tribulation and attacks by false teachers

and worldly prophets, is conquest when it is exercised until the end. The person who exercises this conquering faith is the one who has an ear to hear what the Spirit says to the churches, that is, the word of the gospel.

The outcome of this conquering by faith and perseverance is the reward, although these letters do not specifically call it reward.[6] Every reward described is an aspect of the inheritance couched in terms that are appropriate to the literary style of Revelation, and which use images drawn from the Old Testament: the tree of life, deliverance from death, the hidden manna and a new name, rule over the nations, the book of life, the temple of God, the throne. To conquer is to persevere in the faith, and to persevere in the faith is to do good works in response to the love of God shown to us in the gospel.

To sum up the function of the seven messages, we see that they link the daily existence of every child of God—never in isolation, but always in the context of a local congregation—to the cosmic struggle between Christ and Satan. This struggle, in view of the decisive victory of Christ in his life, death and resurrection, can have but one outcome. Nevertheless the struggle continues until the consummation at Christ's return. Since the age of this struggle lasts from the ascension of Christ until his return, the specific problems of the seven churches serve as representative examples of the daily struggles of all Christians of all ages. We may, of course, approach these messages as warnings to seek to live more faithfully in the world. But, as noted above, the unity of the seven letters with the apocalyptic visions, and thus with the ultimate warfare and victory of the kingdom of God, brings the significance of the two distinct theatres of war together. It is impossible to regard the seven letters as simply preceding the apocalyptic visitations in time. To do this is to trivialize the struggle of each child of God. Rather we see that there is a great mystery here. Christ's "mopping-up" campaign against Satan is actually, marvellous to relate, being worked out in the front-line trenches of local church evangelism, pastoral care, teaching and preaching. It is being

6. But see Revelation 22:12.

worked out in the Christian home as children are instructed in their covenant privileges and taught the meaning of faith in the doing and dying of Christ. God is truly using what is foolish in the eyes of the world to shame the wise, and using what is weak in the eyes of the world to shame the strong (1 Corinthians 1:27). Those who lust for the kind of power that the world respects, who seek to establish before men a triumphal image of the church and of Christian existence, reject the victory of the Lamb at the point of daily living and declare that they are as offended by his suffering as were those Jews who could not tolerate a king-messiah who dies. The gospel pattern of daily Christian existence is one of a confident struggle. When the Spirit of God writes upon the hearts and minds of ordinary Christians the truth that the victory of God, his glory and his majesty, are all clothed in the suffering of the Lamb, he dignifies our struggle with a significance that outshines all the remarkable feats to which the world attaches fame and importance.

Summary

The seven letters to the churches serve to introduce the main themes of Revelation by dealing with them at the outset in the down-to-earth context of the daily life of the local congregations. The drama of redemption is thus shown to have on-going effects in the world of human existence. Christians are not onlookers while a cosmic conflict rages in spiritual realms, but rather they are participants. The letters prevent the apocalyptic descriptions of this spiritual struggle from being detached from our daily struggle. The risen and glorified Christ calls upon his churches to be faithful to his gospel and to persevere in well-doing. During this period of the overlap of the ages the lordship of Christ in the world is expressed through the church which is made up of responsible human beings. The good works which are demanded are part of the apocalyptic struggle with the powers of darkness. Because the final inheritance of Christians follows on a life characterized by good works, it may be spoken of as reward, even though its basis is not those works but Christ's merits.

THESIS

The seven messages to the churches structure Christian existence during the overlap of the ages as a creative tension between the sovereignty of God and the responsibility of man.

6

'I saw a beast coming out of the sea'
The Apocalyptic and Prophetic Passages

And I saw a beast coming out of the sea. He had ten
horns and seven heads, with ten crowns on his horns,
and on each head a blasphemous name. The beast I saw
resembled a leopard, but had feet like those of a bear
and a mouth like that of a lion. The dragon gave the
beast his power and his throne and great authority. One
of the heads of the beast seemed to have had a fatal
wound, but the fatal wound had been healed. The whole
world was astonished and followed the beast.

All the inhabitants of the earth will worship the beast
—all whose names have not been written in the book of
life belonging to the Lamb that was slain from the creation of the world (Revelation 13:1-3,8).

In a book of such diverse literary forms as Revelation, it is
proper at least to ask why the author switches from one style
to another. Why does John start with an introduction which
is heavy with Old Testament allusions and apocalyptic
imagery? Why does he then change to an epistolary (letter
writing) style in the messages to the churches, and then revert
to heavenly visions? Why are sections of apocalyptic visions

interspersed with sections that, although visionary, do not contain such a wealth of apocalyptic symbolism? Can we detect any special reason which makes apocalyptic particularly appropriate to the purpose of the book?

In Chapter 4 I discussed the way that apocalyptic depicts the day of the Lord or the day of the coming of the kingdom. We saw that apocalyptic and prophetic material shared the same general perspective. Both depict the present age coming to end and the new age immediately beginning with the full glory of God's everlasting kingdom revealed. The differences between the prophetic and apocalyptic views of the end lie in the respective emphasis on the extent of the action, and in details. They both have essentially the same perspective as far as the relationship of this present age to the new age goes. The differences in literary style are, for the most part, easy to see, although some prophetic oracles have apocalyptic features. Because prophecy and apocalyptic differ mainly in style, form and emphasis, it is possible to blend the two, or to mingle sections of each, without upsetting the general perspective. What is important for our understanding of how the apocalyptic and prophetic idioms function in Revelation, is that their perspective is that of the straight linear progression from the old age into the new. It is this perspective that I shall maintain is preserved in the apocalyptic-prophetic sections of Revelation.

What then are the apocalyptic sections and how are they connected?

The Vision of Christ (1:12-20)

John begins the book with the words, "the revelation of Jesus Christ". He then tells us that he testifies to everything he saw, namely the word of God and the testimony of Jesus Christ. In his greeting to the seven churches he identifies, and gives glory to, Christ as the source of blessing. But then as he describes what he was told to write and to send to the seven churches, the idiom changes quite dramatically. The one who speaks to him is identified as Jesus Christ only by inference and because of the introductory section preceding. We are told that John sees one "like a son of man". Of course we are familiar with this title as it is given to Jesus in the Gospels. The origin of the title and the significance it bears must be sought in the Old Testament background to the ministry of Jesus.[1] Those references to the Son of Man "coming with the clouds", show the link between Jesus Christ described in Revelation 1:7 and in 1:13:

> Behold he is coming with the clouds,
>   and every eye will see him,
> even those who pierced him (Revelation 1:7).

> and among the lampstands was someone
>   "like a son of man" (Revelation 1:13).

With this we compare a typical passage from the Gospels:

> At that time men will see the Son of Man
>   coming in clouds with great power and glory
>   (Mark 13:26).

The most reasonable assumption is that these references use a concept based upon the apocalyptic vision in Daniel 7. Daniel, one of the Jewish exiles in Babylon during the sixth century B.C., has a vision:[2]

> Four great beasts, each different from the others, came up out of the sea. The first was like a lion, and it had the wings of an eagle. I watched until its wings were torn off and it was lifted from the ground so that it stood on two feet like a man, and the heart of a man was given to it (Daniel 7:3-4).

1. The debate over whether Jesus actually used the title of himself, as the Gospels claim, and if so, what he meant by it, is not really our concern. I must agree with those who accept that "son of man" signified a central participant in the drama of salvation as worked out in the history of Israel. It is clear from Revelation 1:7 that Daniel 7:13 is in mind.
2. Many scholars do not accept that the Book of Daniel was written by or about a sixth century Daniel. It is generally taken to be a second century B.C. apocalyptic work which uses the figure of Daniel, quite possibly an historical person, as the basis for an anti-hellenistic work. In my opinion

Daniel then describes two more beasts, one like a bear, one like a leopard, then a fourth, more fearsome beast appears. It has ten horns and an eleventh appears with the eyes of a man and a boastful mouth. Then Daniel says:

> As I looked, thrones were set in place,
>   and the Ancient of Days took his seat.
> His clothing was as white as snow;
>   the hair on his head was white like wool.
> His throne was flaming with fire,
>   and its wheels were all ablaze.
> A river of fire was flowing,
>   coming out from before him.
> Thousands upon thousands attended him;
>   ten thousand times ten thousand stood before him.
> The court was seated, and the books were opened.

> Then I continued to watch because of the boastful words the horn was speaking. I kept looking until the beast was slain and its body destroyed and thrown into blazing fire. (The other beasts had been stripped of their authority, but were allowed to live for a period of time.) In my vision at night I looked, and there before me was one like a son of man, coming with the clouds of heaven. He approached the Ancient of Days and was led into his presence. He was given authority, glory and sovereign power; all peoples, nations and men of every language worshipped him. His dominion is an everlasting dominion that will not pass away, and his kingdom is one that will never be destroyed (Daniel 7:9-14).

In good apocalyptic style, Daniel is given an interpretation by one standing by:

> The four great beasts are four kingdoms that will rise from the earth. But the saints of the Most High will receive the kingdom and possess it forever (Daniel 7:17-18).

---

the arguments for this view are by no means conclusive and create as many problems as they seek to solve. However, the question is not important for this discussion since the evidence would suggest that Jewish apocalyptic began to develop during the Babylonian exile.

The general significance of Daniel's vision is made clear by the interpretations given (Daniel 7:16-27). The beasts are the godless powers of the nations of the earth. By contrast with the beasts, a human figure comes with clouds of heaven to God and receives the dominion which has been stripped from the beasts. The interpretation either identifies the human figure with the people of God, or implies that he receives the dominion as their representative. The identification of the beasts as godless humanity is not unique to this vision. For example, Psalm 22 is obviously referring to evil men who persecute the righteous complainant:

> Dogs have surrounded me;
>   a band of evil men has encircled me,
> they have pierced my hands and my feet.
> Deliver my life from the sword,
>   my precious life from the power of the dogs.
> Rescue me from the mouth of the lions;
>   save me from the horns of the wild oxen
> (Psalm 22:16,20-21).

It is possible that this approach reflects the fall of man when, because of the sin of Adam, the dominion of man over the beasts (Genesis 1:26) came under challenge. Be that as it may, Daniel's vision speaks of the reversal of the godless power-structures of this evil age. It is significant that it is a human figure that is involved. In this regard, let us remember that "son of man" in Hebrew and in Aramaic (the language of Daniel 7) means no more than "human being", and is here a contrast to the beasts.

Who, then, is the man who has dealings in heavenly places to receive the kingdom for the people of God? The New Testament claims that it is Jesus, our representative and substitute. And John's vision is of the one like a son of man who has all power and who has even assumed something of the appearance of Daniel's vision of God. Furthermore, he identifies himself as "the first and the last", which in Isaiah 44:6 is the self-description of the God of Israel, in order to impress the fact that "besides me there is no god". The son of man is the man Christ Jesus who is also true God.

So much for the background of John's opening vision. But

there is also another remarkable feature. The description "son of man" is thoroughly grounded in Old Testament apocalyptic. In fact this vision contains nothing that is not in the idiom of the Old Testament, except perhaps the references to the churches (in the plural) in verse 20. Then, when we move into the seven messages of this son of man, the author continues to be identified in these apocalyptic terms of the prefatory vision. Again the "churches" remain the only distinctly Christian expression in the seven letters.

The Vision of Heaven (Chapters 4-5)

This prelude to the seven seals begins with a vision of the throne of God in heaven. It is very reminiscent of Ezekiel 1 where the prophet sees strange sights including something not unlike the four living creatures of Revelation 4:6-8. The message of the praise of the twenty-four elders is that God is seen to be Lord because he created all things. Then comes the drama of the seals which only the Lion, revealed as the Lamb slain, is worthy to open. John here does not depart from the apocalyptic idiom and Christ, both as Lion and Lamb, is described in Old Testament images.

The Seven Seals (Chapter 6)

In this section the opening of the seals is, with one exception, the signal for a manifestation of God's wrath. Beginning with the "four horsemen of the apocalypse" the series moves to the description of the catastrophic day of wrath. The four horsemen (seals 1-4) recall, with some significant differences, the apocalyptic passages in the post-exilic prophet Zechariah (Chapter 1:7-17). Again it is noteworthy that this section could be removed from its New Testament context and there would be no clue to its origins in a Christian book. Only the final reference to the wrath of the Lamb might leave a pre-Christian Jew slightly bewildered.

The Sealing of the Multitudes (Chapter 7)

The first part of this vision is also without any overt relationship to the Christian message. It is the perfect number out of the twelve tribes of Israel that is sealed against the impending doom. The only mystery for our pre-Christian Jew would be the omission of the tribe of Dan and the inclusion of Joseph along with the half-tribe of Manasseh.[3] He might wonder if the writer were ignorant of the history of Israel, but he would not thereby discern the hand of a Christian.

The second part of this vision, in which John sees the great multitude gathered out of every nation, tribe and language is no more overtly Christian in its vocabulary than the first part. It contains several references to the Lamb but does not use the name of Christ or refer to his ministry in New Testament terms. The final description of the redeemed (Revelation 7:15-17) is thoroughly Old Testament, borrowing images from the prophets and the Psalms. However, the hymnic section of this vision does provide a gospel-based perspective as we shall see in the next chapter.

The Seven Trumpets (Chapters 8-9)

The blowing of the trumpets unleashes a series of fierce judgments upon the earth and upon mankind. This section is about as typically apocalyptic as it could be. In the whole two chapters there is not one phrase which identifies the material as Christian.

The Angel's Message (Chapters 10-11)

Between the sixth and seventh trumpet this section intrudes as a prelude to the seventh. The angel speaks to the sound of seven thunders and announces that there is to be no more

3. The tribe of Joseph was divided into the two half-tribes of the sons of Joseph, Ephraim and Manasseh. Levi, as the priestly tribe, was given no territorial inheritance in the promised land—see Joshua 13:33,14:4.

delay, "but that in the days of the trumpet call to be sounded by the seventh angel, the mystery of God, as he announced to his servants the prophets, should be fulfilled" (Revelation 10:7 RSV). Then follows a series of allusions to events of the Old Testament. John is told to eat the scroll in a similar experience to that of Ezekiel (Ezekiel 2:8;3:3). Then he is told to measure the temple like the man of Ezekiel's vision (Ezekiel 40:3). He sees the lampstands and olive trees which are similar to those of Zechariah's vision (Zechariah 4:11-14). These are identified as God's two witnesses who have power to do the signs and wonders that Elijah and Moses did. Finally the witnesses are killed by the beast, but they are raised up and taken to heaven. Again except for the reference to the crucifixion in verse 8, this section is pure Old Testament. Only when the seventh trumpet is sounded do we hear a voice in heaven speaking of the fact that the reign of Christ has come (Revelation 11:15-18).

The Beast Visions (Chapters 12-14)

First, John sees warfare between the dragon and the woman who bears a child. The dragon, who is Satan, is thrown down and then a voice declares that the kingdom of God and the authority of Christ have come. Secondly, John sees a beast rising out of the sea. The whole description is very similar to the beast vision of Daniel 7, except that there is only one beast. This beast appears to prevail over the saints and to gain the allegiance of all whose names are not in the Lamb's book of life. A second beast appears to aid the first in his conquest of the world. All men brought under the beast's dominion are marked with his mark.

Then John sees the Lamb on Mount Zion with the 144,000 who are marked with the Father's name. Three angels emerge with stern warnings of judgment. A voice announces the blessedness of these who die in the Lord. The son of man sits crowned upon a cloud, with a sickle in his hand. The time has come for the harvest of the grapes of wrath.

Into this magnificent procession of apocalyptic pictures John injects only the one reference to the kingdom of Christ, but it is thoroughly immersed in the idiom of the Old Testament.

The Seven Bowls of Wrath (Chapter 16)

The pouring out of the seven bowls of wrath brings terrible plagues upon the earth. These are not unlike the visitations of wrath that we have already witnessed. In keeping with the apocalyptic trend of Revelation, this section contains no distinctively Christian terminology at all.

The Judgment of Babylon (Chapters 17-18)

The first part of this section maintains the apocalyptic style. John is shown the great harlot Babylon. She is drunk with the blood of the saints and of the martyrs of Jesus (Revelation 17:6). She sits on a seven-headed beast with ten horns. The angel tells John that the horns are kings that make war on the Lamb but are conquered by him. The second part of this section is marked by a shift into the cycle of prophetic oracles announcing woes upon Babylon. The fact that the historical city of Babylon figures in such Old Testament prophecy, as the evil city of the captivity of the Lord's people, makes the style of those prophets appropriate to this section. All in all only the one reference to the martyrs of Jesus interrupts the Old Testamental style and content.

The Final Visions (Chapters 19-22)

Only in the last group of visions is there a prominence of New Testament themes. But even here they are couched in apocalyptic terms and thus do little to add a gospel perspective to this Old Testament landscape. The first vision of the group (Revelation 19:11-16) presents us with yet another apocalyptic horseman. This time his identity is made clear from the description and, above all, from the name by which he is called: The Word of God. He leads a heavenly army as he rides forth to execute a wrathful judgment on the world.

Next John sees an angel summoning the birds to a feast of the flesh of the mighty men of war. Then the beast and the armies of men make ready to fight against the horseman. But the beast is captured along with the false prophet and they are thrown into the lake of fire. The armies of men are destroyed. The scene shifts (Revelation 20:1-3). An angel seizes the dragon, Satan, and binds him, then throws him into a pit for a thousand years. Then the martyrs of Christ are restored to life and reign with him for the thousand years. When this period comes to an end Satan is loosed from the pit. He gathers his armies for battle against the saints but there is no conflict. Instead fire from heaven consumes them and the devil is thrown into the lake of fire forever. Again the scene shifts to a great white throne of judgment (Revelation 20: 11-15). The dead stand before the throne to be judged and those whose names are not in the book of life suffer the same fate as the beast, the false prophet and the dragon.

Finally, John sees a vision of the new heaven and new earth. He describes the holy city, new Jerusalem, as the dwelling place for God in the midst of his people in the new earth which they have inherited. It is a place that brings together all the blessings that have previously been described as belonging to Eden and the promised land. Now the conflict is ended and the people of God experience only the eternal presence of God and the Lamb.

The Function of the Apocalyptic Sections

What, then, have we learned from this summary of the apocalyptic sections of Revelation? First, we have seen that the apocalyptic has been inserted into a New Testament framework of eschatology. Although some occasional references to Christ and his kingdom occur, they do little more than identify the subject of what is otherwise entirely Old Testamental in both its form and context. The kingdom of Christ is portrayed as coming with the day of the Lord's wrath. The present evil age is terminated on that day. From first this angle and then from that, John paints vivid word pictures of the terrible doom of the day of the Lord. It is a horrendous series of images, each of which defies mere visual reproduction. There is no question of chronological sequences being strictly observed either within or between the several series of visions. No one description or apocalyptic vision can do justice to the all encompassing activity of God as he puts down the cosmic rebellion and saves his people. Every aspect of the created order, from the spiritual powers to the dust of the earth and the uninhabited planets, is caught up in the upheaval of that day.

Secondly, we have learned that the threat of undoing under the weight of God's wrathful judgment has no terrors for the redeemed. They are sealed and kept against that day, which does not spell destruction for them, but resurrection and glorification. No power in heaven or on earth can touch the people of God. They constitute in God's sight a perfect number which he will not suffer to be diminished through misfortune, chance, or onslaught of the devil. What is more significant is that the wrath of God has already been visited upon them in the person of their substitute, the Lamb who was slain. They, united to the Lamb by faith, now live in him and receive the same unqualified approval from the Father as he does.

The overall effect is to depict the tribulation of the day of the Lord which became such a prominent theme in Old Testament prophecy and apocalyptic. Apocalyptic horsemen, trumpets heralding unprecedented destruction, bowls of wrathful judgment, beasts and false prophets overthrown, the saints sealed and secure though tormented for a while by persecutions and martyrdom; all this makes up the scenario of the day of the Lord. On the one hand the battle goes on in the church, on the other it is presented in apocalyptic terms of a struggle that transcends the earthly order and yet goes on being waged on earth. The beast and the dragon, in a foul alliance of spiritual wickedness, manifest their frenzy of hatred of the kingdom of God in the history of the world. The false prophet, and all the accusers and troublers of the suffering church of Christ, gather together all godless humanity for the struggle in what is called Armageddon. Such frightening pictures could easily overwhelm the timid and faint-hearted Christian fighting for survival. But it is not left like that. Wrath is put into perspective by the sealing of the saints. Armageddon is put into perspective by the millennium.

Finally, let us suppose that some of John's readers, then and now, should ask, "When will all these things be?" There is no doubt that for many people the burning questions about the Book of Revelation relate to when the tribulation occurs, when and where Armageddon is fought, when the millennium takes place. These questions on the lips of modern readers are often expressions of a failure to understand apocalyptic and how it operates. By his very use of apocalyptic John has answered all these questions: "These things will be at the *end*, they are the events of the day of the Lord." Only the gospel, which John has carefully built into the book and with which he surrounds the apocalyptic sections, will save us from exasperation at this reply to our question!

Summary

The apocalyptic sections of Revelation maintain the perspectives of the day of the Lord which belong to Old Testament apocalyptic and prophetic writing. As we follow through the visions of Revelation we find that John has found no reason to deviate in any marked way from the portrayal of the linear succession of the two ages. Furthermore, a minimum of distinctively Christian terminology finds its way into the visions. Enough is said to show that Jesus Christ is the central figure in the great conflict between God's kingdom and the powers of darkness which takes place on the day of the Lord. The New Testament perspective of the overlap of the ages is not evident in the apocalyptic visions. Yet the victory is still Christ's. The visions do not present a chronological sequence of events relating to the end of the world. Rather they show a variety of aspects of the final event in such a way as to indicate the different dimensions ranging from the personal struggles of the individual Christian to the cosmic battle in which Satan and all his allies are destroyed. Apocalyptic also provides a strong sense of the sovereignty of

God in our salvation so that every believer may stand confidently in the knowledge that he is sealed against the day of wrath.

THESIS

The Old Testament perspective of the day of the Lord is maintained in the apocalyptic sections. All the events of the end, which in the New Testament are structured by the overlap of the ages, are depicted as occurring during the one undifferentiated day.

7

'Worthy is the Lamb who was slain'

The Hymnic Passages

Worthy is the Lamb, who was slain,
to receive power and wealth and wisdom and strength,
and honour and glory and praise!

Hallelujah!

For our Lord God Almighty reigns.
Let us rejoice and be glad and give
him glory!
For the wedding of the Lamb has come,
and his bride has made herself ready
(Revelation 5:12; 19:6-7).

The Coming of the End

In the last chapter I attempted, without going into a lot of
the detail, to show the emphasis of the apocalyptic visions,
and the perspective they have of the end. To the question,
"When will these things be?", I proposed that John's answer
is, "At the end". We must now attempt to clarify that

answer. Our difficulty lies partly in the fact that the Old
Testament idioms employed by John portray the end as a
single undifferentiated point in time marking the conclusion
of the old age and the beginning of the new. Many Christians
still struggle with the disciples' question in Acts 1:6: "Are
you at this time going to restore the kingdom to Israel?"
They struggle with it because they fail to see that Jesus'
answer, by pointing to the giving of the Spirit at Pentecost,
was thus pointing to the preaching of the gospel as the way
the kingdom would come in the period between the ascension
of Jesus and his second coming.

The main thing that I have been arguing for in this book, is
that the gospel was the fulfilment of the promises concerning
the kingdom of God. It is the gospel which thus restructures
the Old Testament perspective as we have seen in Chapter 4
above. It is, I believe, the loss of the gospel perspective which
has led to so much confusion over the Book of Revelation.
When the gospel is separated from the question of the fulfilment of the promises to Israel, it leaves a void. Jesus Christ
forces upon us the need to interpret the Old Testament, and
all its literary idioms and forms, in the light of the New Testament. But when the gospel and this present "church" age are
interpreted as intrusions between the promises to Israel and
their literal and future fulfilment, then we are in fact interpreting the New Testament by the Old. The gospel is made
subservient to the Old Testament. This ought not to be.

The disciples' question about the restoration of the
kingdom showed two things, one correct and the other that
needed correction. The correct perception of these men was
that the resurrection of Jesus, which restored their confidence
in him as the promised redeemer, signalled that the day of the
Lord had come. They were now at the *end*. Their incorrect
perception was due to their persistence in the Old Testament
frame of mind which saw the single undivided moment of the
transition from one age to the next. We should not be too
critical of this misperception since it would require the events
of the ascension of Christ and the giving of the Holy Spirit to
make clear to the disciples how the gospel, as fulfilment, has
modified or qualified the form of the promises.

The nature of this gospel qualification of the Old Testament perspective has been discussed in Chapter 4; all we need here is to remind ourselves that the new understanding of the end provided by the event of Christ is extremely important. It is vital to our perception of the realities of Christian existence, particularly as this is characterized by a tension within us between the new age, already come in Christ, and the old age which still exists within us and around us.

The subject of this chapter is the way John overcomes the disadvantages which attach to his use of apocalyptic and other Old Testament forms which preserve the simple linear perspective of the two ages. I want to suggest that the Book of Revelation is provided with a framework of explicitly gospel-oriented material which prevents it from being a piece of purely Judaistic apocalyptic as far as its perception of the end is concerned. This framework consists mainly of the hymnic sections or interludes to the visions of the day of the Lord. We may also add to this the introduction and the last of the visions with their distinctly final nature.

All that I have argued for in the first three chapters relates to this dimension of Revelation. Although in actual quantity the apocalyptic visions far outweigh the rest of the material, John has left us in no doubt that the gospel is the heart of all he wants to say. Thus the *end*, as John sees it, is primarily the end come in the historic events of Jesus of Nazareth. The *end* came for us in the person of our substitute who was content to become the suffering and slain Lamb. His was the great tribulation, his was the victory of Armageddon on Calvary, his was the binding of Satan. This was *the* event which secured for all the saints their inheritance in the kingdom of God. On this basis the pattern of our present existence is shaped. The character of the church is modelled on its Lord. What came in him and was achieved by him for us, patterns the process of reaching the end in us as the Holy Spirit creates and sanctifies the church.

But it is not simply that the church, as the gathering of the saints, is the venue in which each individual Christian is sustained in the personal struggle towards the goal of being like Christ in his present glory. It is also, as we have seen, that until the Lamb is revealed as the Lion, the body of Christ must identify with its head in his character as the Lamb. Thus the church suffers. And yet the Lamb is victorious. So the church, in the midst of its sufferings, can know what it is to conquer.

Not until Christ is revealed in the glory of the Lion shall we be glorified. The day of the Lord remains veiled from sight under the suffering of the Lamb until that time. Being veiled, it is perceived only by the faith that the gospel creates in the people of God. But it is real nevertheless, as everyone who truly believes in the gospel will affirm. The problem of Christian existence is that we easily allow the tribulation which we experience within the suffering church to obscure the glory that is already ours by faith in Christ. This is the problem that the Book of Revelation sets out to rectify. If only that object and aim of the book were kept in mind we could be spared a lot of speculative interpretation. John's first concern is not to minister to armchair prophets in some far-off age, but to the battlers of his own day who struggle to reconcile the fact of their suffering with the fact of Christ's victory over sin, Satan and death. In that concern he is our contemporary also.

The Gospel Framework

The introduction has already been discussed at some length so we need only, at this stage, remind ourselves of the prominence which John gives to the historic gospel in Revelation 1 (see Chapter 3 above). We ought never to lose sight of John's first chapter, especially when we get to the succession of apocalyptic visions. The time element in what John says at the beginning is important. Note the following—
The past:
>Jesus Christ freed us from our sins by his death, and rose from the dead (v.5). He has made us a kingdom of priests to his God (v.6).

The present:
>Jesus Christ is now the ruler of the kings on earth (v.5). He is now also the ruler and guardian shepherd of the churches (v.16,20). He is now alive and will live for evermore (v.18). He holds the keys of Death and Hades (v.18).

The future:
> Jesus Christ is yet to come with the clouds so that
> every eye will see him (v.7). His coming will bring
> consternation among the peoples of the whole
> earth (v.7).

It is no light thing that John describes in greatest detail at
the outset that which is the present reality. The vision of
Revelation 1:12-20 is the vision of the now ruling Christ.
Christian existence is a matter of the present. Of course we do
not live in the present without regard for the past or the
future. But live in the present we must. John writes for the
present in the light of the past victory of Christ, the present
reigning of Christ, and the future consummation of Christ's
rule. And if Christ rules now, then he has overcome his
enemies decisively in the past events of his life, death and
resurrection.

It is central to the gospel as the key to biblical interpretation
that the past event of the finished work of Christ determines
absolutely the nature of the present and the future. This is
why I have said that we may not interpret the New Testament, and in particular the Book of Revelation, on the basis
of the Old Testament perspective. It stands to reason that
since the gospel fulfils and reveals the final significance of the
Old Testament, we must allow the gospel to determine the
meaning of the Old Testament.

In terms of the structure of the Book of Revelation we
observe that the gospel framework is established by the interludes to the apocalyptic sections. The introductory section is
the prelude to the seven letters. The heavenly vision of
chapters 4 and 5 is the prelude to the seven seals. In the first
chapter we looked at the vision of Revelation 5. The Lamb
slain is the only one worthy to reveal the truth of the kingdom. The song of the elders echoes this truth and attributes
this worthiness to the saving acts of Christ:

> You are worthy to take the scroll and to open the seals,
> because you were slain, and with your blood you
>   purchased men for God
> from every tribe and language and people and nation.

> You have made them to be a kingdom and priests to
>   serve our God,
> and they will reign on the earth (Revelation 5:9-10).

Then the angels, the creatures and the elders sing:

> Worthy is the Lamb who was slain,
> to receive power and wealth and wisdom and strength
> and honour and glory and praise (Revelation 5:12).

Notice the emphasis on the past event of the death of Christ as that which creates the present reality of the kingdom of priests which is the church. It is said that the redeemed "will reign on the earth", but this future tense does not imply only a remote future but rather an ongoing reign from the time of redemption. They are *already* a kingdom (Revelation 1:6, 5:10). Neither does it exclude the remote future, for the perspective of the New Testament on what we call heaven or eternal life is of an earthly existence. It will of course be the renewed earth, but earth all the same. Some popular notions of heaven tend to be more pagan than Christian in that they remove the earthly environment and also the bodily existence of the redeemed.

The next interlude occurs in the account of the sealing of the multitude before the visions of the seven trumpets. These are the ones who are guarded against the judgment which is visited upon the earth. They are the justified saints who cry out with a loud voice:

> Salvation belongs to our God
>   who sits on the throne,
> and to the Lamb! (Revelation 7:10)

This is followed by another short hymn ascribing glory to God (v.12). The elder who interprets for John tells him that the multitude consists of those who are coming out of the tribulation (John uses the present tense here). The psalm-like description which follows makes it clear that these redeemed saints did not escape tribulation but rather came through it. The Lamb—who is always for John the Lamb who was slain

—has wrought salvation. Tribulation comes but does not overrun the saints who have washed their robes in the Lamb's blood. The relationship of this vision in time to John's day is not the important thing. What is being depicted here is the three stages of salvation: justification, sanctification (including suffering) and final glorification. This view of the security of the redeemed is not unlike Paul's overview of the unbreakable chain in the process of salvation:

> And those he predestined, he also called;
> those he called, he also justified;
> those he justified, he also glorified (Romans 8:30).

In the passage under review, John describes the glorification of the saints as final deliverance from suffering:

> Therefore they are before the throne of God
> and serve him day and night in his temple;
> and he who sits on the throne will spread his tent over them.
> Never again will they hunger; never again will they thirst.
> The sun will not beat upon them, nor any scorching heat.
> For the Lamb at the centre of the throne will be their shepherd;
> He will lead them to springs of living water.
> And God will wipe away every tear from their eyes
> (Revelation 7:15-17).

The question whether this glorification is intended to be understood as happening now or only after the general resurrection is not the concern of this passage. It is the purpose of this vision to reassure the suffering saints that the past event which brought the Lamb through his suffering death and resurrection to the throne, has fixed once and for all their destiny to be forever with the Lamb in his glory.

The next interlude, between the seven trumpets and the series of beast visions (Revelation 10-11) includes the description of the two witnesses of God whose testimony evokes a fearful attack by the beast. The sounding of the seventh trumpet (Revelation 11:15) brings us to another hymnic section as a prelude to the next series of visions. Loud voices are heard in heaven saying:

> The kingdom of the world has become
> the kingdom of our Lord, and of his Christ,
> and he will reign forever and ever (Revelation 11:15).

Then the twenty-four elders worship God saying:

> We give thanks to you, Lord God Almighty,
> who is and who was,
> because you have taken your great power
> and have begun to reign.
> The nations were angry and your wrath has come.
> The time has come for judging the dead
> and for rewarding your servants the prophets
> and your saints and those who reverence
> your name,
> both small and great —
> and for destroying those who destroy the earth
> (Revelation 11:17-18).

The most logical understanding of these hymns is that they refer to the final glory of Christ's kingdom and to the last judgment. Certainly, if we link them with the preceding description of the two witnesses, this appears to be the case. Thus once again John describes the mission of the church, under attack, but victorious. The "two witnesses" vision is, as we saw in the previous chapter, almost entirely lacking in specifically Christian terminology. The witnesses are described as Old Testament prophets. Only the reference to the place "where their Lord was crucified" (verse 8) shows them to be witnesses to the gospel. Like their Lord they are killed, and like their Lord they are raised and taken to heaven. Then the kingdom of Christ is announced. The two witnesses are a description of the present church age which is characterized by conflict and persecution. John's interest in martyrs is born out of the reality of his day. The death of the witnesses does not thereby mean the obliteration of the church at some point in this world's history. John reassures his readers that even martyrdom cannot overcome the power that raised Jesus. The description is too reminiscent of the suffering, death, resurrection and ascension of Christ to be accidental. Once again the church is reminded that its character and experience must reflect the character and experience of her Lord. The singling out of martyrdom does not remove this passage from the sphere of every Christian's experience. Again there is an affinity with the message of Romans 8:

> As it is written:
> "For your sake we face death all day long;
> We are considered as sheep to be slaughtered."
> No, in all these things we are more
>   than conquerors
> through him who loved us.

(Romans 8:36-37[1])

The prelude to the seven bowls of wrath includes the song of the saints who have conquered the beast (Revelation 15). Before the last plagues are announced these saints are seen by the sea of glass mingled with fire. The next reference to their song as the song of Moses and the Lamb perhaps suggests that the sea represents the trial that they have passed through, just as Moses led Israel through the Red Sea. There Israel witnessed the saving acts of God in wrathful judgment on their enemies. Moses sang a song praising the triumph of Jehovah the divine warrior. Now, in John's vision, the saints sing the song of Moses and the song of the Lamb:

> Great and marvellous are your deeds,
>   Lord God Almighty.
> Just and true are your ways,
>   King of the ages.
> Who will not fear you, O Lord,
>   and bring glory to your name?
> For you alone are holy.
> All nations will come and worship before you,
>   for your righteous acts have been revealed.

(Revelation 15:3-4)

1. William Hendriksen has caught the spirit of John's message in the title of his exposition of Revelation—*More than Conquerors* (Grand Rapids: Baker Book House, 1939).

Although it is called the song of Moses, this hymn has little verbal similarity to the song of Moses in Exodus 15, except perhaps in the phrase:

Who is like you—
   majestic in holiness,
awesome in glory,
   working wonders? (Exodus 15:11)

The main similarities lie in the perspective of salvation. The song of Moses recalls the objective acts of God in history whereby he saved Israel. That event foreshadowed the true and spiritual exodus achieved by the Lamb, the mediator of the new covenant. The great and marvellous deeds, of which the saints of John's vision sing, are the objective historical events of the gospel. The day of the Lord came in the person and work of Jesus Christ.

Then we were told that those who sing this song are those who have been victorious over the beast. According to the seven messages to the churches this is the victory of the life of faith and perseverance, but made possible only because of the victory of Christ. Thus the day of the Lord comes also in and through the life of the church in the world as it makes the gospel known. The saints of this vision have finished their struggle and have entered into their reward. The fact that this is portrayed before the last plagues should not concern us. The pattern of apocalyptic in general, and of Revelation in particular, does not require a strict chronological sequence. It is quite appropriate for John to depict the saints in con-summate glory before describing the final tribulation of wrath. For one thing, Revelation is clearly not in strict chronological order; there is repetition. For another, the nature of the end as the gospel defines it makes it difficult to define from the apocalyptic passages, any reference to one, and only one, aspect of the coming of the end. For John to refer to the seven last plagues does not mean that they occur only at the point of Christ's return.

After the pouring out of the seven bowls of wrath the inter-lude includes the apocalyptic description of Babylon the harlot city (Revelation 17), and the prophetic oracle on the

downfall of Babylon (Revelation 18). Then comes the hymn
of the great multitude in heaven:

> Hallelujah!
> Salvation and glory and power belong to our God,
> for true and just are his judgments.
> He has condemned the great prostitute
> who corrupted the earth by her adulteries.
> He has avenged on her the blood of his servants
> (Revelation 19:1-3).

Later John hears the voice of the great multitude again:

> Hallelujah!
> For our Lord God Almighty reigns.
> Let us rejoice and be glad
>   and give him the glory!
> For the wedding of the Lamb has come,
> and his bride has made herself ready.
> Fine linen, bright and clean,
>   was given to her to wear (Revelation 19:6-8).

Having emphasized many times that the tribulation of the last
days cannot overcome the saints, John also speaks of the fact
that the enemies of the kingdom of God, the godless powers
of the world, are doomed to suffer utter destruction. Once
again the overall perspective is included. Babylon has been
the persecutor of God's people. The apocalyptic struggle has
ever characterized this day and age of grace. The history of
the true church is sprinkled liberally with the blood of
martyrs. The justice of God may seem to be a pipe dream to
the down-trodden and the persecuted. But it is real. "Vengeance is mine, I will repay, says the Lord" (Romans 12:19,
RSV). When this vengeance is finally visited upon the godless,
the marriage feast of the Lamb will have begun. The gospel
age will inevitably give way to the final destruction of
Babylon which heralds the consummation of the kingdom.

Before we come to the epilogue (Revelation 22:6-21), we
should note some of the distinctives of the last group of
visions. In many respects this group (Revelation 19:11-22:5)
shares the same characteristics as all the other apocalyptic

visions. As we saw in Chapter 6, the form and style continue to be predominantly Old Testamental. Christ, rather than the Lamb, is specifically mentioned with regard to the millennial reign (Revelation 20:4-6), but the perspective is unchanged. However, when we come to the vision of the great white throne (Revelation 20:11-15) and the vision of the New Jerusalem (Revelation 21:1-22:5), there is an increasing sense of the finality of the end. The lake of fire is described as the second death, and Death and Hades are consigned to it. This finality has been anticipated in the casting of Satan into the lake of fire forever (Revelation 20:10). From this point on, the description is not of an undifferentiated end but of the consummation. In many respects this finality must be inferred from the fact that John allows no more place for suffering or for the onslaughts of the devil. The promises and purposes of God are fulfilled:

> Now the dwelling of God is with men, and he will live with them. They will be his people, and God himself will be with them and be their God. He will wipe every tear from their eyes. There will be no more death or mourning or crying or pain, for the old order of things has passed away (Revelation 21:3-4).

This final version will be considered in more detail in Chapter 9. Here let us note that even if John continues the apocalyptic style, as he clearly does, we may expect some indication that the consummation is a reality to which all things eventually come.

Finally, the epilogue brings us back to the present. No more apocalyptic visions here, only the reality of Christian experience in the here and now. There is an urgent call to face the reality that *now* is the end. In the older apocalyptic style the writer was told to seal up in a book that which was revealed to him. There it would remain until the appointed time of the *APOCALYPSIS*, the *revelation*. The seals would be broken and the secrets of the visions revealed. This would be the time of the end. But the angel says to John, "Do not seal up the words of the prophecy of this book, because the time

is near" (Revelation 22:10). There is no time to seal it and lay
it aside for the future. As John writes down the visions it has
been granted to him to see, at that very moment, the end is
upon the world. Furthermore, while the tribulation of the
end may last for years, everyman's consummation lurks
around the corner of his life. For in the moment that he
thinks not, the evil man is caught in the midst of his evil-
doing, the righteous man taken in the midst of his right-doing
(v.11). Then, irrespective of the centuries, even millennia,
that will pass before the universe is caught up in the consummation, each will find that there is no more time. Christ's
coming is for each of us as close as the moment of our own
death. Blessed indeed are those "who have washed their
robes, that they may have the right to the tree of life"
(Revelation 22:14).

Summary

While the apocalyptic sections speak of the end of this age
in the manner of the Old Testament, John fits them into a
framework of passages which impress the gospel perspective
upon us. The end is the end as it came for us in the person of
Jesus Christ. The end is the end as it goes on coming in the
church. And the end is the end as it will come in consummation at the return of Jesus Christ. This perspective is
provided principally by the hymnic interludes between the
apocalyptic visions. Only in the last section of apocalyptic
visions is the gospel perspective of the interludes reinforced.
Here John explicitly resolves the ambiguities that exist in the
other apocalyptic sections. That is, he makes it quite clear
that the overlap of the ages is no more. The devil is finally
removed forever and the new age emerges alone as that to
which the saints are finally conformed.

THESIS
*The Old Testament perspective, which remains unmodified
in most of the apocalyptic sections, is modified by the gospel
framework in the introduction, interludes (hymnic sections),
and in the epilogue.*

8

'And there was war in heaven'
Conflict and Armageddon

And there was war in heaven. Michael and his angels
fought against the dragon, and the dragon and his
angels fought back. But he was not strong enough, and
they lost their place in heaven. The great dragon was
hurled down—that ancient serpent called the devil or
Satan, who leads the whole world astray. He was hurled
to the earth and his angels with him (Revelation 12:7-9).

Conflict is Inescapable

In Chapter 2 we considered the reality of suffering as the
normal experience of Christians in the world. We saw that
what Jesus said about the matter was very relevant to the
theme of Revelation: "In the world you have tribulation, but
be of good cheer, I have overcome the world" (John 16:33).
Now I want to take an overview of John's use of the conflict
theme in Revelation. Conflict and tribulation are related very
closely in the biblical picture of the coming of the kingdom of
God. In the Old Testament direct causes of suffering and disruption are often stated without analysing the total picture of

the origin of evil in the world. But if we are prepared to allow the essential unity of the Bible we may arrange the evidence into an overview of the situation. Revelation follows the kind of dualism which develops in Old Testament apocalyptic. That is, we observe a conflict between light and darkness, good and evil, God and Satan which may be thought of as taking place in the spiritual sphere or heavenly places, but which also has its outworking in the affairs of men on earth. One immediate and exciting implication of this is the fact that the affairs of the church in the world have cosmic effects. We tend to think of our personal struggle and the struggles of the church as nothing more than the residue of the blight of sin. Yet Paul, for example, reminds us that the struggle is with spiritual powers (Ephesians 6:12).

It would not be true to say that conflict occurs only because God has refused to allow Satan's challenge. The deists believed in a god who withdraws from the world and is no longer interested in it. Such a withdrawal could not prevent conflict, for creation can be in harmony only when related to God. Some conflict then is the direct effect of sin which destroys proper and harmonious relationships within creation. The God of the Bible is not the god of the deists. He has not left the world to its own devices. Nor has he allowed Satan to steal his world. Rather he has challenged Satan's claim, and invaded his usurped domain in the person of Jesus Christ. Every saving act of God is a direct rebuke to the devil. *The* saving act of God was the living and dying of Jesus Christ. This experience of the slain Lamb was the definitive conflict by which redemption comes to all the people of God.

By entering into the human realm, into our human existence, through the incarnation, Christ entered into the realm of our slavery to Satan. He must either conquer or submit. In his very being he constituted the kingdom of God for he was both God and man relating in perfect harmony. For Christ to have submitted to Satan is as unthinkable as God abdicating the throne of heaven and allowing Satan to take his place as ruler of the universe. The incarnation of Christ was the necessary pre-condition to salvation. It was the focusing of the area of God's action into human existence. This is where it had begun. Since man had been created as the pinnacle of all creation, Satan attacked the kingdom of God at that point. He had decided to get at God through man. The temptation of Eve and the subsequent sin of our first parents was, to all appearances, Satan's victory over God's kingdom. Sin and death came by man, and likewise righteousness and life must come by man:

> As one man's trespass led to condemnation for all
> men, so one man's act of righteousness leads to
> acquittal and life for all men (Romans 5:18, RSV).

> For as by man came death, by a man has come also the
> resurrection of the dead (1 Corinthians 15:21, RSV).

What we often forget is that, just as the sin of Adam had cosmic consequences, so also the salvation of Christ has cosmic consequences. The whole of creation is involved in both situations. In other words, just as the sin of man led to the disruption of the whole universe so the righteousness of Christ leads to the restoration of the whole universe. And this does not happen apart from us. The redemptive suffering of Christ occurs in the field of conflict between God and Satan. Christ's death on the cross was, in fact, his victory over Satan. It was his victory over every demonic power which enslaves us. The miracles of Jesus in which he casts out demons are indications that the messianic mission must include victory over that dimension of reality.

The conflict between God and Satan has various dimensions to it which belong to the nature of things as the Bible reveals it. Paul's use of the analogy between Christ and Adam is very important. Romans 5 is the main passage which expounds this relationship. Most people can grasp the idea that Adam was the man who brought sin into human existence, and Christ was the man who dealt with the problem. Adam was tempted and sinned, thus bringing mankind out of the garden paradise into the wilderness. Christ came into that wilderness, was tempted and withstood the devil, thus making open the way back into paradise. Paul's argument, however, is a little more involved than that. He is saying that Adam represented all humanity so that his sin was our sin. In like fashion Christ represents the whole of the new humanity so that his righteousness is our righteousness.

Let us take this argument a step further. Because we all, by virtue of our unity with Adam, share his guilt, we then express this original sin by living sinfully. So also, because by virtue of our faith unity with Christ we are accounted as righteous as he is, we then go on to express this righteousness in our lives. Of course we do not express it perfectly because of the sin that will remain until we are fully redeemed. The point is that the life of man is a reflection of what he is in his representative head. If we are Adam's then we express Adam's nature. If we are Christ's then we express Christ's nature. It has been emphasized constantly in this study that the Lamb stamps his character upon the body of those united to him by faith. That is, the church assumes the character of its head. The Lamb's conflict with Satan is also a suffering and redemptive act. That is why the church will go on suffering until the Lamb is revealed in all the glory of the Lion.

A further implication of this is that the representative and substitutionary suffering of the Lamb, which is *the* conflict with Satan, goes on being reflected in his people. The church's suffering and conflict with Satan reflect that great battle which climaxed in Calvary. What happened in the person of our representative head for us, is reflected in our lives until the consummation when the final cleavage comes and evil is put away forever.

The Conflict for our Justification

The conflict motif, like every other aspect of God's saving acts, belongs to all three dimensions of salvation: justification, sanctification and glorification. In this regard the New Testament shows the onslaught on demonic powers and their overthrow depending upon the first of these dimensions which is the gospel. Jesus' victory over the demons, as recorded in the Gospels, is central to the motif of conflict. For example, in Luke 11:14-23 we have the record of the casting out of a demon, which caused the opponents of Jesus to offer the illogical argument that Jesus was in league with the devil:

"By Beelzebub, the prince of demons, he is driving out demons". Obviously Satan does not set out to wreck his own domain. "But", says Jesus, "if I drive out demons by the finger of God, then the kingdom of God has come to you." It is probable that Jesus uses this unusual metaphor for the power of God (*hand* and *arm* are more frequently used to denote power) to recall the event when the magicians of Pharaoh were forced to admit defeat before the superior power of Israel's God (see Exodus 8:19).

The conflict motif in the Gospels presents us also with the discomforting fact that all mankind is caught up in the war between Christ and Satan. In the exorcism just referred to Jesus goes on to say, "He who is not with me is against me, and he who does not gather with me, scatters" (Luke 11:23). This is pointedly directed at those bystanders who accused him of using demonic powers to cast out demons. In Mark's account the accusation is linked with the blasphemy against the Holy Spirit (Mark 3:29-30). In another place Jesus says to his opponents, "You belong to your father, the devil, and you want to carry out your father's desire" (John 8:44). The demonic hold over mankind is nowhere more sensationally revealed than in the confession of Peter at Caesarea Philippi (Matthew 16:13-23). Peter confesses, "You are the Christ, the Son of the living God." Jesus replies, "Blessed are you, Simon son of Jonah, for this was not revealed to you by man but by my Father in heaven." Only God could give a sinful man the eyes to recognize his Christ. But this same man is still capable of thinking like a sinful human. The Christ of God must die to redeem us. "Never, Lord!" says Peter. The rebuke from Jesus must have cut him to the quick: "Out of my sight, Satan! You are a stumbling block to me; you do not have in mind the things of God, but the things of men." The unpalatable truth is there: when a man recognizes the Christ it is by the grace of God. When he thinks like a man he is the emissary of Satan.

So the pattern develops. Jesus brings redemption and the kingdom of God. He does this only by paying the price of his own suffering and death. He casts out demons only because he has deflected the arrows of Satan's temptations in the wilderness, and is set to run the course of total obedience to his Father's will. The mystery of iniquity is such that we cannot understand why Satan both seeks to divert Jesus from his redemptive suffering and also remains the agent of that suffering (see Acts 2:23). We do know that the conflict was decided by that redemptive act of Christ: "Having disarmed the powers and authorities, he made a public spectacle of them, triumphing over them by the cross" (Colossians 2:15). Of his coming death Jesus said: "Now is the time for judgment on this world; now the prince of this world will be driven out. But I, when I am lifted up from the earth, will draw all men to myself" (John 12:30-33). The gospel is the power of God to overcome the powers of evil. The disciples received a foretaste of this as the seventy were sent to preach the good news that "The kingdom of God is near you" (Luke 10:8-18). When they returned rejoicing that even the demons submitted to them, Jesus said, "I saw Satan fall like lightning from heaven."

The Conflict in our Sanctification

We have established that Satan gained his hold over the universe through his entry into the arena of human existence. The redemptive act of God, like a surgeon's knife attacking a deadly cancer, must take place in the same arena. Christ's justifying work in his living and dying included his victory over Satan's power in the world. The structure of salvation has been adequately discussed in previous chapters, and this structure is now applied to the area of Christ's victory over Satan. What Christ did for us has its outworking in all believers as sanctification. What we already are in Christ (victorious over Satan) begins to take shape in our experience as the Holy Spirit conforms us more and more to the reality which is in Christ. The Christian struggle is against the world, the flesh and the devil.

When Paul concludes the Ephesian letter by turning from the practical issues of life (Ephesians 5:1-6:9) to the matter of spiritual warfare (Ephesians 6:10-18), he does not take up a new subject. The practical matters of daily life in a hostile world *are* the spiritual warfare against principalities and powers. In urging us to put on the full armour of God, Paul is not departing from the perspective that is consistently his, namely that, by standing firm and clinging to the truth of our justification, we live the life of sanctification. The gospel at work in the believer, in the congregation of believers, is the demonstration to all the spiritual powers that Christ has triumphed (Ephesians 3:10-13).

The Conflict of Glorification

The question as to why the decisive defeat of Satan at the cross was not also his final destruction is the same as the question in Acts 1:6 about Christ restoring the kingdom (see Chapter 7). It has pleased God in his wisdom to bring many sons and daughters to glory through the preaching of the gospel in this present age. Peter describes it as the forbearance of God giving opportunity to people to repent. "But", he says, "the day of the Lord will come like a thief" (2 Peter 3:8-13). The day of the Lord is, in this context, the consummation of the kingdom. The consummation of Christ's victory will be the final and complete abolition and destruction of Satan. But this can be only because Christ has already won the victory over Satan on the cross. The final overthrow is not some new redemptive work of God. It is the outworking of the victory of the cross in the whole universe as God makes all things new. When Satan is thrown into the lake of fire (Revelation 20:10), all conflict, suffering and death cease forever and ever.

The Conflict in Revelation

With this general overview of the spiritual warfare, what shall we make of the motif of conflict in the Book of Revelation? Let us first summarize the conflict as it occurs throughout Revelation.

*The church in the world described in the seven messages
(Revelation 2-3)*

Each of the messages describes some aspect of the struggle.
It is not a passive suffering, but one born out of the conflict
that comes from declaring oneself for Christ. Persecution is
the work of the devil:

> You did not deny my faith even in the days of Antipas
> my witness, my faithful one, who was killed among you,
> where Satan dwells (Revelation 2:13, RSV).

> To the rest of you in Thyatira, to you who do not hold
> to her teaching and have not learned Satan's so-called
> deep secrets ... Only hold on to what you have until
> I come (Revelation 2:24-25).

> I will make those who are of the synagogue of Satan,
> who claim to be Jews though they are not, but are liars—
> I will make them come and fall down at your feet and
> acknowledge that I have loved you (Revelation 3:9).

Others struggle against the enemy within, against immorality,
false doctrine and against lethargy and complacency in the
church. But to all is given the promise that the final blessing is
for him who overcomes, who conquers in this unremitting
warfare against the world, the flesh and the devil.

God in conflict with a sinful world (Revelation 6-7)

The opening of the seals leads to terrible judgments on the
created order. This is the ultimate manifestation of the curse
of Genesis 3. But the saints are sealed against this judgment
by the redemptive work of Christ. Otherwise they would be
caught up in the destruction.

The same kind of conflict is found in the visions of the
trumpets (Revelation 8-9). The horror that is released here is
that to which mankind has submitted in its rebellion against
the creator. The devil has no designs to be a beneficent ruler
but only to destroy. There is divine irony in the fact that the
powers of darkness actually serve the purpose of God to
bring about their own undoing.

The beast emerges as the adversary of the church (Revelation 11)

The preaching of the gospel by the two witnesses is stren-
uously opposed by the beast from the bottomless pit. The
witnesses suffer a fatal blow and there is rejoicing in the earth
at the apparent defeat of God's people. But the resurrection
of the witnesses is accompanied by a terrible retribution upon
their foes. The heavenly choirs sing praises to God, for his
kingdom has overcome the powers of the world.

War in heaven and earth (Revelation 12-14)

The apocalyptic description of the dragon persecuting the
woman with child (Revelation 12:1-6) shows the interrelation-
ship of the spiritual powers in heavenly places and the earthly
conflicts involving the people of God. What happens in
heaven is inextricably bound up with what happens on the
earth. Then there is war in heaven between Michael and the
dragon. Satan, the dragon, is defeated and thrown down to
the earth. That his downfall is due to Christ's redemptive
work, rather than some primaeval fall of Satan from being a
servant of God, is clear from the interpretation given by the
heavenly voice:

> Now have come the salvation
>   and the power and the kingdom of our God,
>   and the authority of his Christ.
> For the accuser of our brothers,
>   who accuses them before our God
>   day and night,
> has been hurled down.
> They overcame him by the blood of the Lamb
>   and by the word of their testimony.
>   (Revelation 12:10-11)

Thus the heavenly and angelic battle corresponds to the
defeat of Satan by the conquering saints who overcome by
the conquest of their saviour and substitute, Christ.

Then John sees a vision of two beasts who represent the
dragon and exercises his authority to deceive people and to
cause them to worship the beasts. People who do not worship
it are slain. All the followers of the beast are marked with a

human number—**666**. But then there is the glorious vision of
the Lamb on Mount Zion with all that belong to him, who
are marked with the Father's name. Two angels flying in mid-
heaven call upon the dwellers of the earth with the message of
grace and the message of judgment. A third angel utters a
warning of the fearful consequences of worshipping the
beast. "This", says John, "calls for patient endurance on the
part of the saints who obey God's commandments and
remain faithful to Jesus" (Revelation 14:12). Then the scene
changes and it is not the Lamb, but the visionary son of man
from Daniel 7, who begins the harvest of the grapes of wrath.

The bowls of wrath (Revelation 16)

Again we see God in conflict with his rebellious creation.
The earth has become the domain of the beast, the arch-
enemy of God. As in the previous visions of the seals and the
trumpets, the curse of God on creation is extended to these
terrible acts of judgment that overtake the children of Adam
who have chosen to become the children of the devil. The
connection between the devil and the sinful world is clear
from the fifth bowl poured out on the throne of the beast so
that men gnawed their tongues in agony and cursed the God
of heaven (Revelation 16:10).

Once more we see the powers of darkness rushing to bring
about their own downfall. The sixth bowl of wrath stirs
demonic spirits to assemble the godless powers of the world
for the battle of the great day of God the Almighty. This is
Armageddon. The final bowl of wrath is poured on Babylon,
the symbol of all Satan's strongholds among men.

The death of Babylon (Revelation 17-18)

The seventh bowl is a prelude to a more detailed description of Babylon's overthrow. Babylon is "the great harlot"—
the biblical image for idolatry and apostasy. She is drunk
with the blood of the saints. World powers make war on the
Lamb but are overthrown by the Lamb. Then the logic of evil
emerges again as the beast wars against the harlot (Revelation
17:16-17). Evil cannot preserve order but only consume it. It is
the judgment of God which condemns evil to self-destruction.

The divine warrior of the Lord's day (Revelation 19-20)

John's vision of the rider on the white horse is magnificent and terrible. He comes to smite the nations with the sword of his mouth and rule them with a rod of iron. This universal lordship is revealed in his name: King of kings and Lord of lords. Again the spiritual conflict is one that has its out-working on earth. The beast gathers the forces of the kings of the earth to war against the divine warrior. There is a terrible slaughter and the beast and the false prophet are thrown into the lake of fire. Now we come to that controversial passage about the millennium (Revelation 20). John sees an angel take Satan and bind him in the pit for a thousand years. The martyred saints come to life again and reign with Christ for the thousand years. Then Satan is loosed from the pit to gather his forces for battle against the saints. But there is no contest, for fire from heaven consumes the enemy. Then the devil is thrown, finally and forever, into the lake of fire. The conflict is ended. There remains only the judgment at the great white throne which separates the redeemed from the lost. Heaven and earth pass away and eternal day dawns on the new heaven and new earth, the dwelling place of God, the Lamb and the multitude of the redeemed.

Conflict in Apocalypse and Gospel

We must now try to bring some order out of this series of expressions of the spiritual conflict. The gospel must be allowed to be the key to our understanding. There is no reason to suppose that John has a very different perspective on the conflict from that of other New Testament writers. Indeed we have observed how he treads the same paths of gospel-centered thinking. Allowing for the apocalyptic perspective in the Book of Revelation is crucial at this point. In other words the great apocalyptic struggles involving the dragon, the beast, the false prophet and the kings of the earth against Christ and his saints, depict the coming of the day of the Lord. The groups of visions repeat the same theme over and over again, looking now at one aspect, now at another. I must repeat that the question about when all this comes to pass can be answered only by reference to the end. We should always try to put ourselves into the shoes of the Jew nurtured on the Old Testament when we read the apocalyptic visions. For him the end was a single event. All the various facets of the terrible conflict and the spectacular victory of the divine warrior belong to that day.

Furthermore, we do an injustice to the apocalyptic way of thinking when we treat its method of reckoning time in a modern scientific way. In our discussion of the Day of the Lord we noted that the Bible deals with time in terms of both its quantity and its quality.[1] We are used to the former with our exact reckoning of years and months. But with our scientific bias towards exactitude we can easily grow impatient with the Bible's apparent slackness over details. The constant repetition of rounded numbers—forty years in the wilderness, forty days being tempted, seventy years of exile, and so on—suggests a rather different approach to the quantity of time. More significant, however, is the qualitative use of time. Here it is not the exact amount of time that elapses that really matters, but the quality of events which characterize the time: So Christ's coming can be pegged to a series of identifiable historical events and people (Luke 3:1-2) and thus be related to quantitative time, or it can be described as the event which gives time its meaning (Galatians 4:4). The qualitative aspect can be seen also in Peter's rejection of the relevance of quantitative time with regard to the period between the first and second comings (2 Peter 3:8-10): "With the Lord one day is as a thousand years".

Apocalyptic takes the concept of qualitative time to its high point by the symbolic use of numbers to express, not literal quantities of time in days, months, and years, but the quality of the time. The quality of the time is determined by the significance of God's action within it either to save or to judge. It was a failure to allow for this that gave strength to the scoffers who taunted the early Christians over their expectation of the imminent return of Christ (2 Peter 3:3-4). "Where is the promise of his coming?" they asked. If God

1. See p.63. See also Simon J. De Vries, *Yesterday, Today and Tomorrow* (Grand Rapids: William B. Eerdmans, 1975).

promised a "day of God" on which all the prophetic words about the coming of the kingdom will come to pass, how is it that he still has not appeared in his reigning glory? (And if this was the problem in the *first* generation of the church, how much more now in the twentieth century?) Peter shows us in that context that *the day* of the Lord is not confined to a quantity that we can discern as so many days or years or even millennia. But, it is still the day of God's action to bring in the kingdom. Of this new age which has intruded into the old through the coming of Christ, Paul says, "This is the appointed time, this is the day of salvation" (2 Corinthians 6:2).

That the new age has invaded the realms of the old age is the cause of the apocalyptic conflict. But let us be clear about the perspective the gospel gives to this. As we have seen, the Old Testament views the two ages consecutively:

$$\text{Old age} \longrightarrow \begin{array}{c} \textit{Day} \\ \textit{of the} \\ \textit{Lord} \end{array} \longrightarrow \textit{New age}$$

The New Testament modifies this by showing that all the ingredients of the end are there in the gospel. Man's sin is judged in the person of Christ on the cross. The new humanity is resurrected in Christ and ascends to the right hand of God. Satan is confounded and cast out. His power is removed by the finger of God. The decisive conflict has taken place and the kingdom of Christ is victorious. The old age goes on but it can never be the same again. All history subsequent to the death and resurrection of Christ is history at the end.

All "A.D." history is in crisis because the Holy Spirit constantly reapplies the decisive victory of Calvary and the empty tomb through the preached word of the gospel. Goliath is vanquished and now the people of God, armed with the victory of their king, great David's greater Son, storm the cities of the Philistines with the invincible weapon of the preaching of the gospel. And it is not only evangelism that pillages the strongholds of Satan, but the ongoing battle to bring every thought captive to obey Christ (2 Corinthians 10:3-6). The conflict is in the sanctification struggle precisely because this struggle is the new age taking hold of us who were formerly children of the old.

The consummation will mean the removal of the last vestiges of the old age. If there is to be some last great conflict it will be the prelude to the universal unveiling of the new age in all its glory. The consummation will mean that what we actually are in ourselves will finally coincide with what we are in the person of our representative and substitute at the right hand of God.

Thus, what the Old Testament apocalyptic portrayed as the single event of the day of the Lord is described in the apocalyptic visions of Revelation from various angles. No one word-picture could suffice to convey the totality of the brilliance and the gloom, the glory and the horror, the joy and the dismay of the day of the Lord. Each series of visions is built upon by the next until the desired effect is achieved. Let me emphasize again that Revelation was written, not for the arm-chair prophets with their charts of historical events in the twentieth century and their intricate diagrams of the end of the age, but for the harassed subsistence-level first-century Christians of the Asia Minor province. It was written to bring them both warning and reassurance, to encourage them in their struggle and to liberate them from fear of the enemy within and without. With a genius for composition that is nowhere surpassed in the biblical literature, John's inspired mind leaves no stone unturned, and yet avoids the unnecessary and obscuring details that so many modern readers wish to read into him. The message comes to us in unfamiliar dress, but that should not be taken to mean that it is impossibly complex.

For these first-century Christians the conflict was real to the point of threatening their very lives. Nor is this to imply that persecution and martyrdom belonged only to the first century. The curious view that most of Revelation is really relevant only to those who live immediately prior to the second coming of Christ makes nonsense of John's concern for his contemporaries, and of the undying relevance of the message throughout the whole of this A.D. age in which the people of God struggle against the foe and eagerly await the Lord's coming.

So when is Armageddon? When are the great conflicts and judgments of John's visions? Again we answer, "At the end." They are the events of the day of the Lord. The day of the Lord is past, for Christ has died and Christ has risen. The day of the Lord is present, for Christ makes himself to reign on this earth through the preaching of the gospel. The day of the Lord is future, for Christ will come again. Armageddon is Calvary. Armageddon is every conquest of the gospel as it shines into this darkened world. Armageddon will be the final putting down of this evil age and its deceitful master. And insofar as we contemplate the possibility of the horror of World War III, we should recognise that its potential for the self-annihilation of our civilization is only a more drastic form of the confusion of evil by which it consumes itself. That confusion has already been given its definitive form at the Cross where evil men were the instruments of Satan's downfall.

The Millennium

The so-called millennium of Revelation 20 is part and parcel of John's dealing with the conflict theme. At the outset I must express my doubts about the attempt to take this symbolic passage and to make a literal description of a future event. In this I am far more in accord with the view known as "amillennialism".[1] It is highly unlikely, to say the least, that something so dramatically significant as a thousand year reign of a reappeared Christ on earth before this age ends should nowhere else be mentioned in the New Testament. The arguments in favour of it depend almost entirely on literalistic applications of Old Testament prophecies in a way that suffers the gospel to be reinterpreted by the Old Testament rather than to have the Old Testament interpreted by the gospel.

See Introduction p.19—amillennialism. This view is expounded in the commentaries on Revelation by Leon Morris, William Hendriksen (*More than Conquerors*), and Michael Wilcock (*I Saw Heaven Opened*). A symposium setting out the different views of the millennium is found in (Ed.) Robert Clouse, *The Meaning of the Millennium* (Downers Grove: Inter Varsity Press, 1977).

That the millennium passage (Revelation 20:1-10) is one of a series of apocalyptic visions cannot be overlooked. That it contains some symbolic material is admitted by exponents of even the most literalistic interpretations. The passage is one which cries out for interpretation. In interpreting such a passage we must allow apocalyptic symbolism to be what it is. Furthermore, we cannot establish a gigantic doctrinal system on one symbolic passage. That is, we must interpret the more obscure passages of Scripture in the light of the clearer ones. Above all the gospel must be our interpretative key: the life, death and resurrection of Christ and all that it achieves for us. The "literalist" position of the premillennial view is, in fact, largely governed by the Old Testament perspective of the linear succession of the two ages. I must point out that there is much Old Testament perspective that premillennialism does not perceive and as a result it maintains its adherence to the impossible principle of literalism. For instance, the pattern of promise and fulfilment in the Old Testament is never strictly literal. The fulfilment of promises always goes beyond the terms of the original promise. We should not think that the New Testament perspective was totally unprepared for in the Old Testament.

Whatever else we say of the thousand year reign of Christ in Revelation 20, it must be maintained that it is part of the scenario of the day of the Lord. Only by removing this from the victory of Christ in his cross and resurrection is it possible to establish the earthly programme which the premillennialists posit for the future. The idea that resurrected saints and a glorified Christ should return to this earth, as yet not glorified, to rule among people who are bound by non-resurrection bodies, has no support anywhere else in Scripture. This earthly millennium is an attempt to come to terms with a self-inflicted problem; that of two different future hopes. The first is the literal fulfilment of Old Testament prophecy in all its Israelite terms, and the second is the consummation of the gospel. The attempt to combine the two destroys the very principle which made this unlikely marriage necessary. That is, literalism cannot survive because the prophets did not promise a future involving both the literal restoration of Israel *and* the gospel.

The literalist-millennial solution is neither literal nor fulfilment. It is not literal in that it must adjust the Israelite expressions of Old Testament prophecy to include the gospel. The restoration involves Christians as well as Jews, Christ as well as David. The literalism is preserved only at the level of the externals—the land, temple etc. It is not literal in that the climax comes in an age of modern technology and not the primitive world of the Bible prophecy. To say that the prophets wrote in the light of their own age is to give the game away. That is precisely the point! For if modern technology is allowed to qualify the literalism of Bible prophecy, why should not an even more significant development in world history also qualify it? How strange that human technology can be accommodated in the literalist's interpretation of prophecy but not *the* event of all history: the gospel.

The literalist millennial view is not fulfilment because its exponents rightly perceive that it does not go far enough. The earthly restoration does not satisfy the millennialist's Christian instincts. So he must have a literal (so-called) fulfilment which is only temporary and which will give way to a permanent gospel consummation. The prophets foresaw an earthly restoration lasting forever. The premillennialist must curtail it in order to allow an even more perfect kingdom to come. The one thousand years of Revelation 20 is thus eagerly grasped as a description of the earthly fulfilment. This ignores the fact that the prophets said "forever" not a thousand years. It also ignores the fact that Revelation 20 says "a thousand years" but says nothing about a bodily presence of Christ on earth during this period.

I conclude that the premillennial solution to Revelation 20 overrides almost all the principles of sound interpretation. The whole structuring of the end-time by the gospel which is the warp and woof of Revelation—not to mention the rest of the New Testament—must be suddenly suspended at this point if the premillennial system is accepted. When we allow the clearer meaning of the gospel to govern our interpretation we are reminded that the life, death and resurrection of Christ establish the pattern of all the saving events. What will happen finally and perfectly at Christ's coming has already begun with the preaching of the gospel. More importantly, the second coming will mean the universal manifestation of what has already taken place for us in the gospel event.

According to this passage, the millennium is the day of the Lord, the day on which Satan is bound. It is the day of Christ's victory and his reign. In one sense, this is where we came in, for John began this book with his vision of the reigning Christ in glory. It is a reminder that the present conflict is not fatal, but an expression of the reigning with Christ of all who are made a kingdom of priests (Revelation 1:6 cf. Revelation 20:6). The thousand years is, as to quantity, an unknown but perfect period of time. As to quality, it is the exaltation of Christ in his glorious rule. It is the privilege of the struggling Christian to know that his very participation in the struggle and the conflict is a share in the rule of Christ. Once more John encourages the saints by removing their existence from the realm of the purely routine, the humdrum, and the meaningless. He removes it also from the realm of senseless suffering and defeat. He points to the fact that in the here-and-now every Christian can know that he, as an individual, has meaning; that his personal identity is defined by the gospel. Even world history cannot overwhelm us, for the gospel has transferred the now into the day of Satan's overthrow. The binding of Satan does not imply that there is no evil, no conflict. Rather it is an affirmation that the kingdom of God has come in Jesus Christ and now permeates the world through the church as it preaches the gospel and lives by it.

Summary

Revelation shows the members of the church in all ages that their struggle against the world, the flesh and the devil, is not a trivial nor a private thing. The theme of conflict, which John weaves throughout, draws all the saints into the arena in which the victory of Christ is achieved. As the gospel has structured the theme of the day of the Lord, so it shows that there is but one conflict in which we are all caught up. Initially the conflict was completely worked out in the life, death and resurrection of Jesus. Satan was decisively defeated at the cross. Christ's victory was for us, so that all believers are accounted victorious in him. Then the same conflict is manifested in the life of the church as Christ, through his gospel applied by the Spirit, works to conform the members of his body to his likeness. Finally the conflict is resolved in the consummation. The millennium, as an expression of the victory of Christ, cannot be confined to the consummation or to a period just prior to it.

THESIS

The conflict of the day of the Lord is structured by the gospel so that it characterizes the three dimensions of salvation—justification, sanctification and glorification. All of the conflict relates to all three dimensions.

9

'I saw a new heaven and a new earth'
The Final Separation

Then I saw a new heaven and a new earth, for the first heaven and the first earth had passed away, and there was no longer any sea. I saw the Holy City, the new Jerusalem, coming down out of heaven from God, prepared as a bride beautifully dressed for her husband. And I heard a loud voice from the throne saying, "Now the dwelling of God is with men, and he will live with them. They will be his people, and God himself will be with them and be their God" (Revelation 21:1-3).

Satan's end

Up till now we have been describing the situation during the period of the overlap of the ages. It is a period of tension, suffering and conflict. It is the time of both having and not having. It is the time of walking by faith, in which the believer knows by faith that he possesses all the riches of Christ and that, in the person of his substitute Man, he has already arrived at the goal at the right hand of God. On the other hand it is the time of pressing on towards the mark, of living in hope of the blessed day when we shall actually experience the goal with all the clarity of perception of which our resurrected beings will be capable.

But a hope without a time of fulfilment is a delusion. The Christian hope is no delusion for its first fruits were revealed in history two thousand years ago in the resurrection of Christ. One day the overlap of the ages will be no more, for the old age will perish by fire. All that belongs to the old age will perish in a death more terrible than death and the great deceiver will be cast into the lake of fire. How can this final transition of the ages be presented in apocalyptic imagery which has not normally been accommodated to the overlap perspective? If the general apocalyptic perspective of the linear succession of the ages has prevailed up to now in John's use of this particular literary form, can it now signify unambiguously the consummation of the kingdom of God? We have to say that it can: John has done it in Revelation 20-22. He has done it simply by removing the ambiguity of the picture of the end. His series of conflicts and judgments that go before have all been ambiguous enough to be applied to the three-dimensional end demanded by the gospel. Now the ambiguity is pointedly removed and the "end of the end", the consummation, is described.

We look first at how John describes the sequel to the millennium. Satan is loosed from the pit and comes out to deceive the nations and to gather them for battle (Revelation 20:7-10). Their object is to attack the people of God, but before this can happen they are destroyed by fire from heaven. No new or extraordinary suffering of the saints is described. Nor are the saints involved in the final removal of the forces of evil. Some interpretations suffer from the need to project a new order of tribulation for the saints immediately before the return of Christ. This is not demanded by the text, nor, we must add, would it be much comfort for the already tribulated saints that John writes to encourage! This "little while" of Satan's loosing must serve another purpose. First, it expresses the paradox that Satan, though defeated and cast out, remains the adversary who prowls around like a roaring lion, seeking someone to devour (1 Peter 5:8). Secondly, it sets the stage for the final denouement. If we may develop Oscar Cullmann's illustration of the decisive battle and victory day, this is the battle for Berlin.[1] Or again, to change the analogy, it is a kind of "High Noon" show-down when the defeat of the enemy is made both public and ultimately effective. The overlap of the ages is past.

With a final flourish John describes the indescribable. For one last time the apocalyptic genius comes into its own. Weaving together the evocative images of the Old Testament with the distinctive elements of the gospel, John creates a tapestry of incredible brilliance. The garden of Eden, Canaan, Jerusalem, and Jesus Christ as the new temple, are portrayed with a skill that does not allow mere words to exhaust the meaning. It was never given to any other New Testament writer to re-create for us so vividly the riches we possess in Christ.

The Meaning of Heaven

It is significant that John draws upon Isaiah's understanding of regeneration. Too often heaven is looked on as a vague, though happy, realm of formless spirit existence. We may laugh at the commonplace cartoon representation showing people with haloes, wings on their backs, harps in hand, and standing up to their knees in cloud. Unfortunately this is uncomfortably close to many Christians' conception of heaven. It is seen as a kind of un-creation in which we are at last divested of material things and especially the clods we call our bodies. We might be tempted to think that John is using the earthly imagery of the Old Testament on the assumption

---

1. O. Cullmann, *Christ and Time* (London: SCM Press, 1951). Cullmann uses the rather confusing notion that the death and resurrection of Jesus became, for the New Testament, the mid-point of time rather than the end. However, he does avoid the need to talk about the end in three ways as I have done in this study. He uses the analogy of war. The gospel event is the decisive victory, but the war continues until all hostilities are resolved at the end which is then celebrated as victory day. I am suggesting that, if the victory is truly *the* decisive victory, it is in the New Testament perspective the end of the war, not its mid-point. This is so even though the war goes on for some time after the decisive victory.

that we will know how to spiritualize it. But such a pagan approach is truly unthinkable. The New Testament simply will not allow us to abolish so completely what we may call— controversially perhaps—the Old Testament view of heaven, and the reason is Jesus Christ who took upon himself our humanity, including its physical side, forever.

The incarnation of God in Jesus Christ, and his bodily resurrection and ascension, establish an important aspect of the Old Testament view of the kingdom of God. I refer to the physical creation. In the beginning God created the heavens and the earth. The earth with the sky above is what this means. This creation of all that exists is looked upon by God as good. It is destined for corruption through sin and, finally, for the destruction of fire. But as the saving acts of God in time and history within this physical universe project the reality of the kingdom of God, so the universe itself is destined, through renewal, to be a part of that kingdom. This is the framework for the biblical doctrine of regeneration.

Let us look at it another way. When God created the heavens and the earth and set man in Eden, man's nature was to relate to God, to his fellow man, and to animal and physical creation. Sin disrupted these relationships so that what God had generated (created) now degenerated. Death settled over the creation. The gospel, however, was in God's mind from before even the creation of the universe, as the means by which all things would be regenerated or re-created. All the Old Testament images of the salvation of God's people involved the re-establishment of the intended relationship between God, mankind and the rest of creation. Man was created a physical being in a physical environment. This in no way detracts from the truth that he was also created a spiritual being in a spiritual environment, that is, in relation to God.

Thus every Old Testament image of salvation included the regeneration of the physical as well as the spiritual. For Noah there was the stark reality of a totally enclosed mini-world in the ark. For Abraham and his Israelite descendants it was the fruitful land of Canaan as the new garden of Eden for the people of God. In the prophets the same Israelitish environment is projected as a future attainment in which the full glory of God's kingdom will exist and yet in a physical environment. Salvation means *all* relationship restored and this includes not only moral regeneration but physical and mental. Sickness will be no more, grief and suffering will be banished. Righteousness will rule the people. The wolf will lie down with the lamb. The desert will blossom as the rose.[2]

Not only is the fruitful Eden image perpetuated, but also the religio-political structures of Israel are established as the model of the future kingdom of God. As David was anointed as the king and his son promised the throne forever (2 Samuel 7:11-14), so it is a new David who will rule in God's kingdom. The temple becomes the focal point of this rule, for it, like the tabernacle before it, represents the dwelling of God amongst his people. The kingdom of God will centre upon the restored and glorified temple on Mount Zion. It is Ezekiel's beautiful image that John recreates in Revelation 22. Here (Ezekiel 47) we see the temple as the source of all life. From God's dwelling flows the river of life which supernaturally increases as it goes. It turns the desolate Arabah region—the valley of the Dead Sea—into a new garden of Eden.

No consideration of heaven is complete without this total regeneration of heavens and earth. We see that the actual word *heaven* has a dual significance. It is first the word for the sky above and, perhaps, the universe beyond. As such it is simply the indispensable canopy for the physical world in which we live. It is used in this sense in Genesis 1:1, Isaiah 65:17 and Revelation 21:1. But Old Testament man also came to recognize that since God is greater than the earth which he made, he must dwell beyond the sky. Thus heaven comes to mean the place "out there" where God dwells. " 'Heaven is my throne and the earth is my footstool' says the Lord" (Isaiah 66:1).

This transcendent "out there and wholly other" view of God is not allowed to remain unqualified. For from the beginning, in the relationship between God and man there is intimacy as well as awe of the transcendent. Adam and Eve

2. See e.g. Isaiah 11:1-9, 35:1-10, 65:17-25. Ezekiel 36:33-36. This is discussed in greater detail in *Gospel and Kingdom*.

"heard the sound of the Lord God as he was walking in the garden in the cool of the day" (Genesis 3:8).[3] God never ceases to be the God who dwells in heaven "out there" (Psalm 20:6, Deuteronomy 4:39, Job 22:12, Psalm 14:2, 33:13, 57:3, 80:14, 102:19). But he is also the God who is "down here". This is not the immanent God of pantheism which removes the distinction between God and creation. It is a saving act of God by which he reaches into our sin-laden existence to establish once again the true relationship between God and man. This is indicated in the placing of the tabernacle in the midst of Israel as the tent-dwelling of God (Exodus 25:8, 29:45-46). In the later history of Israel the moveable tabernacle gives way to the temple in Jerusalem. Because of the relationship between God and man that the temple represents, it is not surprising that it is elevated to great prominence in the prophetic view of the coming of the kingdom of God.

The temple as the sign of "God with us" becomes closely related to the human agent of God's rule. David's son will build the temple, says the prophet Nathan (2 Samuel 7: 12-13). This same Davidic prince is called the son of God (v.14)—a title which identifies him principally as the true representative of Israel (cf. Exodus 4:22-23, Hosea 11:1). But the royal prince is also Immanuel—God with us (Isaiah 7:14, 9:6-7). It is not surprising then, that the New Testament combines all these images in the one person Jesus Christ. He is the true temple (John 1:14[4], 2:19-22). He is the son of David who is also the son of God (Luke 3:22-38).

To return now to the question of the meaning of heaven. The fact that Jesus Christ is now at the right hand of the Father in heaven, and that he has gone to prepare a place for us in the Father's house, does not mean that our final destiny is to be separated from the physical universe. Jesus has taken

3. This translation of the NIV correctly brings out the fact that the verb is singular and refers to God "walking", not Adam and Eve. This example of anthropomorphism—that is, speaking of God as if he were human—enhances the "down here" emphasis concerning God.

4. John 1:14. The word became flesh and dwelt among us. The Greek word translated "dwelt" is a word derived from the word tabernacle or tent.

his own body to heaven. In that is bound up the redemption and renewal of the physical universe. It is in keeping with the scriptural perspective that John sees the new heaven and the new earth, and that the new Jerusalem comes down out of heaven from God. We need not suppose that this is meant to convey a literal descent of the city out of the sky. It is the final touch to the regenerating work of God. It establishes the kingdom which is not from this world. The heavenly country which Abraham longed for (Hebrews 11:16) is not a land in the sky, but a tangible dwelling for redeemed mankind and one in which the people of God will relate truly to God, mankind and the world. It is a dwelling from God, a city from heaven. But when it is set up in the centre of the regenerated earth, it will mean that the dwelling place of God is with men. This is how the story began in the paradise of Eden, and this is how it will end in the regained paradise of God's kingdom.

One last point needs to be made in this regard. I have been personally amazed at just how radical a thought the resurrection can be to some Christians. Even many of those who belong to my own (Anglican) denomination, and who say week by week the words of either the Apostles' or Nicene creeds which state explicitly our belief in the resurrection of the body, seem not to have grasped the implication. On the one hand they confess a bodily resurrection, yet on the other hand they so often seem to operate with a Greek pagan notion of immortality of the soul; of a destiny of timeless and matterless eternity in an ethereal spirit state. The fact, which is often overlooked, is that the bodily resurrection of Christ points to our own, and carries with it also the guarantee of the redemption of the whole physical universe.

God and the Lamb

Throughout this study I have referred from time to time to the motif of the Lamb and the Lion in Revelation 5. It provides us with a symbolic representation of the message of the whole book of Revelation. The paradox of the majesty of the Lion revealed in the suffering of the Lamb is the paradox of the conquest of God through our Saviour Christ.

It is the paradox of the church through which Christ conquers the world, a church which can be the agent of this conquest only by reflecting the nature of its head—the suffering Lamb. It is the paradox of individual and corporate Christian existence as every believer engages in the life-and-death struggle against the world, the flesh and the devil, while at the same time rejoicing in the fact that we have already overcome in Christ. It is the paradox of the overlap of the ages in which the kingdom of God, having already broken into this age in Christ, is being formed in us, and yet remains a future event. It is the paradox of the millennial rule of Christ and the "little while" of Satan's loosing.

Is this paradox ever resolved? The answer must be "yes" and "no"—a further paradox! Yes indeed, as we have seen, the old age eventually perishes along with Satan and all things that belong to him. The overlap of the ages will disappear, the tension of Christian existence will be resolved. The church will cease to be the suffering-servant church and be the church triumphant. But there are some paradoxes which will never be resolved. Particularly we note that the triune being of God is a paradox. Three in one is not expressible in human logic. It is the sameness (unity) and difference (distinction) that characterizes God and which will ever characterize him and our relationship to him.

John can express this paradox only in human language. That which he says of God he can say also of Christ. "I am Alpha and Omega, the beginning and the end" (Revelation 1:8, 21:6, cf. 22:13, 1:17-18). The apocalyptic imagery which has so easily portrayed Jesus Christ, or the Lamb, as having separate identity, is not allowed to destroy the central paradox of the Christian faith: God is one and three. The Lamb is one with the Father and the Spirit. Yet the Lamb is not the Father, nor the Spirit. When we, as the people of God, are brought finally to this glorious consummation we shall be perfect but still human. And because we shall be still human there is no reason to suppose that we shall know God as he knows himself. The paradox of God's being is a true and eternal mystery, not merely a reflection of our fallenness. In the kingdom we shall not penetrate the mystery of the Trinity. Our perfected humanity will be precisely that—

humanity and not deity. Perfect humanity will show itself in the way we shall worship at the throne of God and the Lamb. The mystery shall remain an endless source of praise.

One further paradox remains. The constant theme of this study has been the tension between the glory of the Lion and the suffering of the Lamb. In fact, I have suggested that this tension characterizes the Book of Revelation. We might therefore be pardoned for supposing that the consummation would indeed reveal Christ—at last—as the Lion. Yet, when we come to this final scene of the visions of John, to the fullness of the heavenly kingdom, it is the Lamb we find on the throne. Why should this be? And, furthermore, does this fact not rather undermine the thesis of this study?

Let us remind ourselves from whence we have come. John was told that the Lion of the tribe of Judah has conquered and can unlock the mysteries of the kingdom (Revelation 5:5). This Lion is none other than the glorious and exalted Christ the vision of whom caused John to swoon clean away (Revelation 1:17). And yet, when John turns to see this Lion, he is confronted by the Lamb standing as though it had been slain. Now when we arrive at the point at which we might expect to see the Lion, we still see the Lamb. Obviously we have to remember that we are dealing with images. John has provided us with a series of images or word pictures by which he conveys the truth of Christian existence. It is the truly amazing thing about the gospel that the rule of God's kingdom, which the Lion represents, comes through the suffering of the Christ, which the Lamb represents. No one picture can adequately represent these truths. Thus John has given us a series of pictures which show us the reality of the coming of the kingdom from a variety of standpoints.

There can be no doubt, from John's visions of judgment and the overthrow of Satan, that the Lamb indeed rules with all the power of the Lion. From time to time we see this exalted and judging Christ. But John will never let us lose sight of the true source of this mighty rule in the Lamb's suffering. Thus, in the consummation, the kingdom itself and the glory of God will reveal the majesty of Christ, the Lion of Judah. But the people of God will go through eternity worshipping him as the Lamb that was slain. Since the kingdom came by his suffering, it is not possible that the Lamb slain from the foundation of the world should be set aside and, as it were, forgotten. Christ indeed has authority and power and majesty to reign by virtue of his being true God from all eternity. But, in the hidden wisdom of God, he has determined that Christ's rule in his kingdom shall be by virtue of his redeeming love. It is our destiny to be the subjects of Christ, not only because we are his creatures fashioned by the word of his power at the beginning, but particularly because we are his children, redeemed by his life, death and resurrection as the God-man who was and is for us.

Justification to the very end!

One further comment needs to be made about John's way of expounding the justification of the sinner. In Revelation 14:6-12 John describes the messages of the three angels. The first has an eternal gospel for all people in the face of the inevitable judgment. The second tells us that the judgment has already fallen on Babylon. The third warns that those whose allegiance belongs to the beast will suffer his fate. Commentators differ as to the exact nature of the first angel's gospel. The significant thing is that its context is the final judgment. This is closely related to John's continued use of the figure of the Lamb to the very end. Justification which is not with respect to the final day of judgment is a hollow thing indeed. On the one hand the believer is accounted righteous and freed from the judgment on *all* his sins whether past, present or future. On the other hand the believer is constantly exhorted to endurance and perseverance to the end.

The Lamb's presence in the consummation of the kingdom is a timely reminder of this important fact of our justification. How sad it is when the biblical teaching on justification becomes twisted, as it so often does, into a partial justification. Many have taught and accepted a justification that was nothing more than a forgiveness of past sins. They have misunderstood the nature of sanctification. Because of the New Testament exhortations to godly living, and warnings against falling away, they have supposed that our final justification is based upon our own righteousness in Christian living. Having the slate wiped clean when we are converted is really small gain if it then depends on us to provide a satisfactory degree of righteousness to pass on the day of judgment. It further matters little that this righteousness is usually seen to be the result of God's grace at work in us. For unless we can come at last to the day of judgment with the perfection that God's holy righteousness demands, our sanctified lives count for nothing so far as justification is concerned. The results of this truncated view of justification for past sins only are serious indeed. Amongst protestants it leads to either perfectionism (a delusion), or to a legalism which diminishes the righteousness of God to the level of our ability to achieve. In the Church of Rome it is linked with a rejection of assurance and the doctrine of purgatory.

Let us then behold, through John's vision, the Lamb eternally enthroned. Let us glory in the fact that our justification through the merits of Christ will stand firm before the great white throne on the last day. Let us continually praise and thank our God that Christ saves to the uttermost! The saddest sight to behold within the Christian Church is that of people, young and old, whose true conversion can hardly be doubted, and yet who are plagued by uncertainty and lack of assurance. These have lost sight of, if indeed they ever knew about, justification past, present and future. How easily pastors can rob their people of a rich portion of their inheritance, namely confidence towards God during every day of their life, by failing to instruct them carefully on the distinction between justification and sanctification. Satan has worked great mischief among God's people by obscuring this distinction so that many who believe the gospel for their initial salvation begin to trust in their own sanctification for their final salvation. Let the Lamb in heaven remind us that we will live each day and enter finally into the kingdom clothed in his perfect righteousness—or not at all.

The Marriage Feast of the Lamb

The Bible contains a number of marriage metaphors which relate to the kingdom of God. It seems reasonable to suggest that those which occur in the New Testament are based upon the Old Testament idea that Jehovah, the God of Israel, has taken Israel to be his bride. The marriage relationship is descriptive of the covenant bond that God established with Israel (Ezekiel 16:8-14).[5] The most sustained treatment of this theme is given in Hosea 1-3 (see especially Hosea 2:19-20). We may not treat the marriage of Jehovah to Israel as mere metaphor, for according to Paul the relation of Christ to his church is signified by the marriage of husband and wife (Ephesians 5:31-32). That is, human marriage points to, and receives its meaning from, Christ's relation to the church. The idea of the marriage feast is indicative of the celebration of the kingdom of God is used several times by Jesus, though here the emphasis is upon the joy of being an invited guest at the banquet (Matthew 22:1-14, 25:1-13, see also Matthew 9:14-15). There is also the parable of the great feast which Jesus prefaced by the words, "Blessed is he who shall eat bread in the kingdom of God." The emphasis here is upon the feasting as the celebration of the kingdom; it is not a marriage feast (Luke 14:15-24).

So we have two metaphors which point to the reality of the kingdom. First, the marriage of God and his people Israel bespeaks the covenant relationship which, though Israel shows constant unfaithfulness, will one day be established perfectly through the redemption and renewal of the people. Secondly, the fellowship of the meal expresses the unity of God and his people in the kingdom as it also celebrates the joy of the kingdom. Although the Last Supper re-echoed the

---

5. See also Isaiah 54:6. The marriage of God and Israel is often implied by the judgment that Israel, by breaking the covenant and seeking other Gods, has played the harlot: see Isaiah 1:21, Jeremiah 2:20; 3:1-10. In Isaiah 61:10, the marriage garments are images of the righteousness of God which clothes the redeemed. Isaiah 62:1-5 depicts the marriage of Israel as her vindication. Israel is named Hephzibah ("my delight is in her") and Beulah ("married"). Here, vindication and righteousness are the same, and foreshadow justification.

Jewish passover meal and pointed to its fulfilment in the
death of Christ, it had also an important reference to the final
blessedness of the kingdom of God: " 'I tell you', said Jesus,
'I shall not drink again of this fruit of the vine until that day
when I drink it new with you in my Father's kingdom' "
(Matthew 26:29, RSV). We have to allow that these images are
fluid, that is, they are capable of being adapted and changed
in order to suit the required emphasis. The parable of the
wedding feast (Matthew 22:1-14) and the parable of the ten
maidens (Matthew 25:1-13) make no mention of the bride.
The people of God are here represented by the guests. Indeed
this is the emphasis in John's reference in Revelation 19:9:
"Blessed are those who are invited to the wedding supper of
the Lamb." But here the guests are surely not different from
the bride mentioned two verses earlier: "The wedding of the
Lamb has come, and his bride has made herself ready."

So the people of God are both bride and guests! All this
means is that either image alone does not suffice to describe
the relationship of the Christian to his Lord. He is at one and
the same time beloved covenant partner and honoured guest
at the celebration. Both emphases have their part to play in
our understanding of what it means to be God's people. To
these we must add one more image, that of Revelation 21.
Here John sees the new heaven and the new earth and the new
Jerusalem "coming down out of heaven from God, prepared
as a bride beautifully dressed for her husband" (Revelation
21:2). Again, an angel says to John:

> Come, I will show you the bride,
> the wife of the Lamb. (Revelation 21:9)

John is shown the new Jerusalem, and describes its beauty
and magnitude—a cube on a base of some 1500 miles! Jerusalem the city of God, is people. To put it round the other
way: the people of God is where God dwells. This fulfils most
perfectly all that the covenant with Israel was meant to
convey. It is a relationship which can exist because Jesus
Christ himself was the new temple, the dwelling of God with
us. As both God and man he was both God and true Israel.

Thus, as John sees the new Jerusalem descend, the voice
declares:

> Behold, the dwelling of God is with men. He will dwell
> with them, and they shall be his people, and God him-
> self will be with them (Revelation 21:3, RSV).

This one verse could be said to sum up and to contain the
entire message of the Bible. The whole of the history of the
covenant and of redemption lies behind this glorious affirmation. Every aspect of the hope of Israel—covenant, redemption, promised land, temple, Zion, Davidic prince, new Eden,
—is woven into this one simple and yet profound statement:
the *dwelling of God is with men*. In an indirect way John used
the marriage theme to express this relationship. Jerusalem,
not a city of bricks and mortar, but a city of people redeemed
by the blood of Christ, is the dwelling place of God. Everyone who overcomes is a son of God in this city and inherits all
the riches of the kingdom (Revelation 21:7). The symbolic use
of the number 12, signifying the twelve tribes of Israel and
the twelve apostles, and its multiples in the cubed city, point
to the same perfection and completeness that we saw in the
144,000 of the redeemed in Revelation 7.

This personifying of Jerusalem as the bride of the Lamb is
totally consistent with the movement of personification of
other images of the Old Testament hope and notably that of
the temple. The temple, above all, was to signify the dwelling
of God. But, as we have already seen, the temple is fulfilled in
the new temple which is Christ himself. Jesus of Nazareth
was God-man and, as such, he was the tabernacling of God in
man (John 1:14). He declared his body to be the new temple
(John 2:19-21). He now creates the temple by his Spirit as he
indwells the redeemed (Ephesians 2:19-22, 1 Peter 2:4-10).[6] It
is the people who belong to Christ who can be called the
temple since Christ dwells in their midst by his Spirit. So, for
John's new Jerusalem no symbolic structure can displace the
actual visible glory of God dwelling there (Revelation 21:22).

6. Note Peter's use of Hosea's marriage passage in this context of the
temple: 1 Peter 2:10 is a reference to Hosea 2:23 in which the significance of Hosea's marriage is interpreted in terms of God marrying his
redeemed people—see Hosea 2:16,19. Peter thus draws together the
various Old Testament concepts—temple, chosen race, royal priest-
hood, holy nation, God's own people—with this reference to Hosea.

God himself, and the Lamb are there and they are the temple. That is why the river of life must flow from the throne of God and of the Lamb instead of from the threshold of the temple as Ezekiel originally depicted it (Revelation 22:1-2 cf Ezekiel 47). Even Ezekiel's detailed description carries overtones of Eden, watered by the four rivers and containing the tree of life. It was in Eden that God originally established his relationship with mankind.

Summary

The new heaven and the new earth described by John in Revelation 21:1-22:5 is the resolution of all conflict, suffering and meaninglessness in life. There can be no longer any deficiencies in the relationship between God, man, and the created order. The overlap of the ages ceases as this present world order in which we live is removed with all the evil that characterizes it. Through resurrection and glorification the believer is brought fully into the regeneration of all things. The new age alone becomes the reality of his existence. This is the realm in which the effects of Christ's life and death are perceived and experienced in all their fulness. Because we at present perceive it only by faith and live in it through our representative man Jesus Christ, it is not possible for our thought forms and language to comprehend it. Thus John, with the genius of divine inspiration, composes a mosaic of Old Testament images in order to convey the ultimate reality.[7] How much of this section is truly apocalyptic and how much prophetic is a somewhat academic question. For appropriately, at this juncture, we have a synthesis of both kinds of writing along with John's over-arching grasp of the gospel. That it carries on the tradition of apocalyptic symbolism is obvious, but in this case John has created a unique blending of the forms and images of biblical literature. Each image

7. R. H. Charles, *The Revelation of St. John*, I.C.C. (Edinburgh: T. & T. Clark, 1920) Vol. 1, pp lxxv-lxxxii lists some 20 Old Testament passages directly referred to in Revelation 21:1 to 22:5. He lists a further 7 which probably have influenced John in this section.

conjures up entire scenarios of Old Testament prophetic hope and expectation. But the new message is that reality has now replaced hope or expectation. That which the gospel defines as reality will come to pass for every believer. Such hope inscribed on the heart and mind by the Spirit of God has through the ages steeled the resolve of countless little people, ordinary and unremarkable men and women (as the world counts them), to go on looking to Jesus, the Alpha and Omega, the author and finisher of our faith.

THESIS

John finally resolves the tension of the overlap of the ages by unambiguously describing the consummation of the end as that which occurs after the destruction of Satan and all that belongs to the old age.

10

'Come, Lord Jesus'

Living in hope for the future

> Behold, I am coming soon! My reward is with me, and I will give to everyone according to what he has done. I am the Alpha and Omega, the First and the Last, the Beginning and the End.
>
> He who testifies to these things says, "Yes, I am coming soon."
>
> Amen. Come Lord Jesus (Revelation 22:12-13,20).

John's adventure into the heavenly reality of the consummated kingdom could easily stand as a fitting conclusion to this remarkable work. What could be more encouraging for the saints of all ages and of all conditions of life than to read of their coming perfection and bliss? He would be a dull and insensitive Christian indeed who did not feel some fire in his soul when contemplating these concluding words of this vision:

> There will be no more night. They will not need the light of a lamp or the light of the sun, for the Lord God will give them light. And they will reign for ever and ever (Revelation 22:5).

But in the wisdom of the Spirit of God, John's readers are
to be returned to earth! Breathing the unpolluted air of the
new Jerusalem can easily throw us off balance, for the harsh
reality of the ever present corruption of our age could jolt us
out of our reverie with a shock that might easily disorientate
us for a time. After all, this glimpse of heaven has been given
to assure, comfort, and motivate us in the midst of this evil
age. In the first chapters of the book, John has relayed the
messages of Christ to the struggling churches. The reigning
Christ praised, encouraged and warned the churches so that
they would persevere to the end. Now once again there is
warning and encouragement, but this time it is given with
specific reference to the meaning of the Book of Revelation
as a whole.

First, there is a reassurance concerning the testimony of
this book, that it is in fact the testimony of Jesus himself
(Revelation 22:6,16,20). In this John recapitulates the
opening sections of the Book. There the risen and glorified
Christ, ruling in the midst of his churches by his word and
Spirit, is shown to be the author of this revelation. We notice
that there is no room for apologetics in this situation. The
Bible does not argue for the acceptability of its assertions. It
states them as the truth. The reason for this is that primary
assertions of the Bible relating to truth include the inability of
sinful man to perceive truth because he has rejected the
source of that truth, and also the gracious revelation of truth
in the person of Jesus Christ. As to the mystery of how or
why the godless and rebellious mind, incapable of perceiving
the truth, will then respond to the truth as it is in Christ, the
Bible resolves it in terms of the power of the gospel and the
regenerating work of the Holy Spirit. As to the mystery of
why some who hear the gospel respond and believe while
others reject the truth, the Bible gives the ultimate choice to
God according to his sovereign purpose of election. The cynic
may regard the assertion of Revelation 22:6, "These words
are trustworthy and true", with as much acceptance as he
would regard the smooth assurances of a confidence trick-
ster,—"Lady, would I lie to you?" But the believer knows
them to be the words of the Lord himself and receives them
with well-founded confidence. They are the words of Jesus

Christ the faithful witness (Revelation 1:5). Everyone must face eventually the question of absolute and ultimate truth. Since it is ultimate truth there is no greater or more basic truth by which it can be tested. If it is to communicate itself to us as the truth it must authenticate itself in terms of itself. There is no apologetic for ultimate truth. It simply takes hold of us and brings us into submission. To submit to the ultimate truth is to be blessed (Revelation 22:7).

Secondly, John recapitulates the stern warnings of Revelation: "Do not seal up the words" (Revelation 22:10). The apocalyptists of the past used the literary technique of describing a sealed book written in a bygone age but opened at the appointed time that all may be revealed. This is what lies behind the breaking of the seven seals[1] (Revelation 5:1-8:1). But now the day of revelation has come. Jesus Christ has come in the flesh and we have entered the last days. "The time is near" thus signifies that the consummation of all things is the last remaining move for God to complete the work of salvation. Since the gospel has brought us to the last days there is no room for complacency about the final manifestation of God's glory. It can come at any time and therefore we can only exhort people to make ready for it by responding to the gracious offer of the gospel. We can be sure of this, that at a time which we do not know, the final event will overtake us. Whether it is by our own death or by the return of Christ in glory, the end result is the same—all opportunity to change our minds and to receive salvation will have passed. "Let him who does wrong continue to do wrong" (Revelation 22:11), points to the time when opportunity for repentance is gone. John is not saying that the time

---

1. In the popular Jewish apocalyptic not found in the Bible, the writers claimed that a great figure of the past, such as Moses or one of the twelve patriarchs, was the author. The work was sealed up and is only now, in the writer's time, opened to reveal the truth. Hence the revealing angel is characteristically seen to command that it be "sealed up" (see also Daniel 12:4). It is significant that in the Book of Revelation John is not the author of the truth under the seven seals, but in good apocalyptic style, the seals are broken and the truth revealed. John is not allowed to seal anything up since the day of revelation has come with Jesus Christ.

has already come, for the word of invitation is still given—
"Whoever is thirsty let him come" (Revelation 22:17).

But let those who wish to live godless lives be warned. The
gospel is the great divider as well as the great unifier. The
conflict between Christ and Satan which has characterized
the whole of Revelation still has its outworking in the daily
existence of men and women. The relationship of good works
and salvation that we discussed in Chapter 5 is recalled in the
words of Jesus in Revelation 22:12. "I will give to everyone
according to what he has done", does not refer to good
works as earning salvation, but to good works as the fruit of
salvation through faith.

The final warning is at the end of the chapter and concerns
the "prophecy of this book" (Revelation 22:18-19). Again
the reason for the strong warning is that these are the words
of Jesus Christ, the Lord of the church and ruler of the kings
of the earth. The essence of the warning does not concern the
actual details of the Book of Revelation as such. To add to,
or to subtract from this prophecy means to reject the testimony of Jesus Christ to himself and to his gospel. It means,
therefore, to reject Jesus Christ and his claims over us as the
ruling Lord. Contrary to some popular distortions of the
gospel which see accepting Christ as Saviour and accepting
him as Lord to be two quite separate things, we see that to
believe in Christ for salvation means, among other things,
that we acknowledge him as Lord.

Thirdly, John recapitulates the blessings of the kingdom of
God. "Blessed are those who wash their robes, that they may
have the right to the tree of life and may go through the gates
into the city" (verse 14). The theme of justification fittingly
moves the book to its close. Remember that John writes to
the persecuted minority, the Christians of Asia Minor. What
encouragement can be given them for the moment? The stir-
ring message of Revelation needs to be distilled into a form
that will sustain them in the moment as well as in the long
term. They need to be reminded again that the power of God
for salvation is the gospel of our free justification in Christ.
They need to be undergirded by the truth that their transitory
existence is but a part of the whole range of human history,
and that Christ is Lord over all of it. "I am the Alpha, and

the Omega, the First and the Last, the Beginning and the End'' (verse 13).

So John brings his readers back to the point where faith simply acknowledges, ''God rules and I am his child through the merits of Jesus Christ.'' The children of the kingdom eagerly await its appearing. Meantime they seek to live as true subjects of that kingdom. Such a life of faith is one lived out between the time of the Lamb slain, and the time of his coming in the majesty of the Lion. Nor is it only, or even primarily, the suffering of the Christian that makes him long for the return of his Lord in glory. For, as Saul of Tarsus learned, the persecution of Christians is the persecution and rejection of the Lord: ''Why do you persecute me?'' We long to see our Lord known no more as the humiliated Jesus of the gospel, but as the Lord of glory. We shall be restless until the holy name of our God and Saviour is vindicated, every tongue stopped, and every knee made to bow in acknowledgement of him.

The world looks on the slaughtered Lamb with pity, disdain and even abhorrence. Through the tinted glass of self-importance it views his sacrifice as a joke, or as the natural end of an outmoded ethic based in superstition. But the world itself gives the lie to its own interpretation. For had the Lamb provided such a senseless life and death, the remedy would be to leave it alone to fester and wither away. But the Lamb would not go away. Instead of a few bleached bones and the smell of putrefaction he left an empty tomb and his Spirit who so seared the truth of the gospel into the hearts and minds of his little band of followers that they began to turn the world upside down. For this the world will not forgive him. It rises up and lashes out at the Lamb while pretending that he isn't real. It does this because the one whose spirit pervades the world knows full well that the slain Lamb is his downfall.

The Christian looks at the Lamb and sees the judgment of God on his sin borne by his substitute. But he sees far more than that. He sees the unending glory of the Lion. He can never see the Lion without seeing the Lamb, and he can see the Lion only by beholding the Lamb. So it will be through all eternity. In this life it is faith alone which perceives these realities, and there is a deep longing within every child of God for faith to be turned into sight. When we are captivated by the gospel, we become more and more impatient with our lack of conformity to the reality of the kingdom. We are offended by the world's rejection of our Lord. We long to be rid of the daily struggle in a world that has the smell of death hanging over even the most sublime beauty of creation.

We cannot but yearn to see all things new. To that end we cry: "Come, Lord Jesus."

Appendix:
What is the Mark of the Beast?

Many readers will be familiar with a popular interpretation of Revelation 13 which, I believe, has received far more attention than it deserves. The critical nature of our times, with their uncertainties, global crises, and threats of the imminent collapse of our social structure and economic systems, has created a thirst for anything that can remove the unpredictability of the immediate future. This thirst has encouraged the spread of certain views among Christians which I firmly believe to be a diversion from the central message of the New Testament.

These views are sometimes grouped under the label "futurism" because their common assumption is that Revelation in particular, as well as the Old Testament prophecies of the coming new age of the kingdom, refer almost exclusively to the future end of this present era. It is also generally assumed that modern history, especially since the return of the Jews and the formation of the State of Israel in 1948, points infallibly to the fact that this age is rapidly drawing to a close. The literalist approach to prophecy and Revelation is usually applied in such a way that exponents claim to see all around us the evidences that the second coming of Christ is very close. Despite the fact that Jesus warned against trying to predict the time of his return, many interpreters are making predictions. These predictions are often rather cagily put ("by 1984" or "within this decade") in a way that suggests a sore conscience for trying to do what Jesus said could not be done. Other predictions are more confident, and the passage of time has revealed many for what they are.

Recently there has been renewed interest in a part of Revelation which has always been a point of some controversy. From earliest times the mark of the beast in Revelation 13: 16-18 has received attention from many interpreters proposing solutions to the enigma of 666. Because the Hebrews and Greeks both used certain letters of their alphabets to represent numerical values, it has been commonly assumed that 666 must be the total of the numerical values of the letters in a man's name. The possibilities are legion, and if the Greek version of a favoured name, for example "Emperor Nero" does not add up to 666 then conversion into the Hebrew form has often produced the desired result. In more recent times a similar method has been used to identify the beast as Muhammed, Martin Luther, Napoleon or Hitler. Many Christians, by contrast, have preferred a more symbolic approach to that of numerical equivalence. If we allow that the Bible frequently uses the number 7 to signify perfection, then 666 can be seen as representing a repeated falling short of perfection or "failure upon failure upon failure".

Now a new kind of interpretation is receiving a great deal of publicity. This approach, unlike the other interpretations, takes the number 666 quite literally and, like the Nero-Hitler interpretations, relates them very precisely to the present day. It is claimed that the mark of the beast—the number 666—is emerging in modern society in a way that shows that we are on the verge of a global economy controlled by Satan. Computerised credit is seen as gradually replacing the use of money so that in time—probably a relatively short time—we will become citizens of a world-wide cashless society. The power behind this will be the antichrist who will demand the submission of all people. Already we are gearing up for all this with the use of plastic cards and electronics. Rows of parallel black lines imprinted on supermarket commodities enable prices to be read and recorded electronically, and are a further proof of the approaching time of total control over buying and selling. When that time comes only those who submit to the mark of the beast, a personal, computerized identification number, being imprinted on the right hand or forehead, will be permitted to buy or sell. Thus Christians who refuse to worship the beast and to receive his mark will undergo a very severe persecution.

The general thrust of books which take this line is to impress upon the reader that the time is near and there is consequently a great urgency for response to the gospel. Such response will not, on some interpretations, remove the threat of this persecution for Christians are said to live through some three-and-a-half years of it before Christ takes them up out of this world. Other interpretations see this "rapture" occurring before the final tribulation in which case there is an added incentive to respond to the gospel and so to escape the tribulation.

How seriously this matter is taken by some people is indicated by a question I was asked at a church-sponsored seminar on this subject. The questioner asked, "What will happen if, when the cashless society comes as fulfilment of prophecy, some Christians accept the mark of the beast without realising what they are doing?" There was an obvious sense of foreboding that many Christians will be ignorant of the meaning of Revelation 13 and will walk into the trap of being marked with the beast's mark. In answer to the question I first pointed out that there was a gratuitous assumption in the assertion that the cashless society alone fulfilled this prophecy. There was, furthermore, a complete failure to relate this apocalyptic picture to the clear teaching of the gospel. The result was an unnecessary fear that some Christians would forfeit their salvation because they lacked the right kind of prophetic instruction with regard to Revelation 13.

In the light of the principles set out in this book, there is a much more satisfactory interpretation which does not clash with the teaching of the New Testament epistles. The vision of the beast in Revelation 13:11-18 is one of a series of pictures of the conflict between light and darkness. The beast is an emissary of Satan in the conflict. He deceives many people so that they give allegiance to him, and he actively persecutes the people of God. The nature of apocalyptic does not demand that a literal economic and commercial persecution (verse 17) be posited. On the other hand it is not an impossible fulfilment since political oppression by totalitarian regimes easily carries over into the market place. It is wrong, however, to make that the only fulfilment on the grounds of an apparent correspondence to contemporary events. Such interpretation is aided by a literalistic approach to the beast's mark (verses 16-17), which supposes that we will one day be required to have our identifying number actually imprinted upon us. Of course, as with so much literalistic interpretation, it tends to break down under its own weight. For, if we follow verse 18 strictly, then every single individual will be stamped with exactly the same mark, six hundred and sixty-six, which has value only to identify the members of the group but not to distinguish one from another.

Again the two principles put forward in the introduction are relevant. First, we must reject any attempt to turn a symbolic piece of apocalyptic imagery into a literal description of an event utterly remote from John and his contemporaries. The fact that John refers to the mark of God in the adjacent vision should assist us. I suggest there is a deliberate contrasting of the two situations which is not unlike that of Revelation 7 (see chapter 3 above). Both Revelation 7 and Revelation 14 refer to the 144,000 redeemed saints in contrast to the reprobate who come under judgment. The mark of God in Revelation 14:1 signifies that these are securely sealed as the Father's own possession. No one supposes that to be a child of God we must have a literal mark on our foreheads. It symbolizes the redemption which is received by faith, and sealed by the Spirit of God. Similarly, the mark of the beast must symbolize unbelief, rejection of Christ and his gospel. It is sad that many Christians are being led to think of their eternal security as depending not upon the finished work of Christ for them but upon their prophetic astuteness in discerning the supposed relationship of the beast to the development of a new global fiscal system. Truly, the gospel and the glorious truths of our justification are becoming clouded by this modern fad.

A further implication of the thesis of this book needs mentioning here. The futurist approach which gives a literalistic interpretation and builds on it a prediction about the return of Christ this year, next year or whenever, will of course one day be right! But it will be for the wrong reasons. In the same way it is possible that many of these contemporary events which are seen to be fulfilment of a prophetic word are just that. If the cashless society comes in the way suggested it may well fit the meaning of Revelation 13. That is not really the point at issue. My argument with this line of thinking is that it uses a rather forced approach to demonstrate that the prophecies are being literally fulfilled by these contemporary events for the first and only time.

The misunderstanding here is twofold. First, the concept of signs of the times is often employed in relation to fulfilled prophecy, or in relation to prophecy that is supposedly in the process of being fulfilled. It is assumed on this view that the signs are discernible, once-for-all fulfilments which indicate that the end is near. On this basis approximate predictions of the time of Christ's return are often made. The second misunderstanding relates to the concept of the end which is exclusively applied to the second coming. I have been at pains in this book to point up the three-fold way that the New Testament speaks about the end. On the basis of this biblical perspective I believe we must come to the following conclusion: the signs belong to the whole period of the last days from the first advent of Christ until his return. Their purpose is not to help us predict, contrary to Jesus' warning, the time of his return, but to characterize this whole period as the end time from the perspective of which the return of Christ was as imminent for the apostles as it is for us. John's apocalyptic vision of the beast and his mark belongs to the whole period also, and may have many individual or continuing manifestations. Above all we must not remove this prophecy from the framework of the teaching of the New Testament in general, or from the rest of the Book of Revelation (for example, in its teaching on perseverance to the end). To do otherwise is to add to the gospel and to imply that "faith alone" and "Christ alone" are principles which will not operate at the very last days of this age. It seems, we are being told, that we must add to them a course of action based on a narrow prophetic interpretation. The only consistent way to deal with Revelation 13 and 14 is to see the mark of the beast as characterizing godlessness and faithlessness, while the mark of God characterizes the sealing of those who through faith in Christ are saved eternally.

Index of Subjects and Names

Index of Subjects and Names

Index of Bible References

Index of Bible References